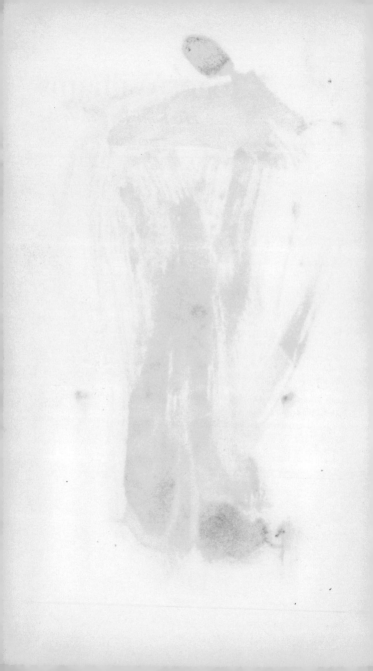

Roger Williams

His Contribution to the
American Tradition

Roger Williams

His Contribution to the
American Tradition

by Perry Miller

Atheneum *New York*

1962

FOR MORTON AND LUCIA WHITE

Published by Atheneum
Reprinted by arrangement with The Bobbs-Merrill Company, Inc.

Copyright 1953 by The Bobbs-Merrill Company, Inc.
All rights reserved
Printed in the United States of America by
The Murray Printing Company, Forge Village, Massachusetts
Bound by The Colonial Press, Clinton, Massachusetts
Published in Canada by McClelland & Stewart Ltd.

First Atheneum Edition

Foreword

POSSIBLY no figure out of the American past today enjoys a greater prestige than Roger Williams—and for none is esteem based on so little familiarity with his deeds or so comprehensive an ignorance of his words. All but one of his books were hastily put through the press during his two brief and crowded returns to London; not only are they now so scarce that they can be consulted nowhere but in special libraries, but they are, even by the baroque standards prevalent during the English Civil Wars, egregious examples of slipshod printing, eccentric spelling, wild use of italics and of barbarous paragraphing. Scholars familiar with seventeenth-century style have difficulty with them, while for the ordinary reader, even if he can come on them, they present formidable terrors. Although most of them were reprinted in six volumes by the Narragansett Club between 1866 and 1874, that edition slavishly followed the originals; moreover, it also has become a rarity. Such of Williams' letters as survive have been printed by scholars intent on exact reproduction; since he wrote them at headlong speed, often without light or a table, they too require infinite patience to decipher.

It rapidly became clear, as I started preparing these selections, that some editorial correction would in any event be required. (Williams' printers, for instance, failed to complete many of his parentheses.) But soon I perceived that my responsibility to Williams went much farther: I had an obligation to make him as readable as possible. I was encouraged because Professor Winthrop S. Hudson gave us, in 1951, *Experiments of Spiritual Life & Health* in a modern format, and the results fully justified him. Even more was I heartened by Samuel Eliot Morison's success in restoring William Bradford's *Of Plymouth Plantation* to literature; in frank emulation I likewise offer a modern but definitely *not* a modernized text. The words on the page are exactly those of Williams, with the omission of a few such distractions as his nervous habit of tacking "&c" to the ends of his sentences, some parenthetical Biblical references and some merely local interruptions. Major excisions are indicated by the conventional ellipses (...), but for those of a word or a line I have assumed that the reader is too intent on the discourse to care. Otherwise, in matters of spelling, capitalization, punctuation and abbreviation, I have exercised the prerogative of a modern editor. I have striven to produce a text as clear as is consistent with absolute fidelity to the language Williams actually wrote. Titles, however, I have kept in their original form.

The greatest of Williams' efforts, *The Bloudy Tenent* and *The Bloody Tenent yet More Bloody*, belong to an age when disputation stretched out interminably, when no controversialist dared to rest until he had refuted every most minute point of his antagonist. Because Williams elected to cast his forensics in the form of dialogues, they are more confusing, and for long stretches more tedious, than even the average polemic of the time. To extract the great and memorable passages calls for something resembling quarrying, and I have shamelessly done just that. Some good passages I have had to sacrifice to the limitations of space, but the gist of his argument, as also the essence of his other works, is, I believe, fairly represented. It must be confessed that Williams did himself great harm by the profusion of his rhetoric; my fingers have long itched to prune his lushness and to help out his heaped-up parallels by the dash—a typographical device of which he was sadly unaware. The opportunity given by this series is therefore most welcome, and I take particular pride in being permitted to present Roger Williams to the America of today.

I have long been persuaded that accounts written within the last century created a figure admirable by the canons of modern secular liberalism, but only distantly related to the actual Williams. I discovered that my feeling was shared by Mr. Mauro Calamandrei, who came fresh from Italy to the study of Williams and who, in an article, "Neglected Aspects of Roger Williams' Thought" (*Church History*, XXI, 1952, 239-258), fortified my resolution to cut through the fog of adulation to the much greater—although often more puzzling —human being who founded Providence and who fought the fight for freedom by his own lights and not by anybody else's.

Cambridge, Massachusetts, 1953   PERRY MILLER

Contents

Chronology

1603—Death of Queen Elizabeth; accession of James I; probable date of Williams' birth

1620—Landing of the Pilgrims at Plymouth

1621—Williams student at Charterhouse

1623-1629—Williams Charterhouse scholar at Pembroke Hall, Cambridge

1625—Accession of Charles I

1629—Williams becomes chaplain in household of Sir William Masham at Otes, Essex; March 4: charter of the Massachusetts Bay Company; December 15: Williams marries Mary Barnard

1630—The "Great Migration" to Massachusetts Bay; December 1: Williams and wife leave England

1631—Williams lands at Boston (February 5); refuses offer of Boston pulpit, prevented from accepting a call from Salem, goes to Plymouth

1633—Williams minister in Salem

1635—Controversy with colonial authorities; October 9: Williams sentenced to banishment

1636—January: Williams flees from Massachusetts; Summer: settlement of Providence

1636-1637—Pequot War

1637-1638—Antinomian crisis in Massachusetts; Anne Hutchinson and Antinomians remove to Rhode Island

1639—Williams temporarily a Baptist; becomes avowed "Seeker"

1642—Civil Wars begin in England

1643—Williams in London as agent of Rhode Island

1644—March 14: Parliamentary charter of Rhode Island; July 15: publication of *Bloudy Tenent*

1649—January 30: execution of Charles I

1651-1654—Williams' second trip to London

1652—Publication of *Bloody Tenent Yet More Bloody*

1654-1657—Williams "president" of Rhode Island

1660—Restoration of Charles II

1663—Royal charter of Rhode Island

1668-1670—Controversy between Rhode Island and Connecticut over the "Pequot lands"

1672—Williams' debate with the Quakers

1675-1676—King Philip's War

1683—Death of Roger Williams

I The Natural Man

ROGER WILLIAMS was born, probably in 1603, in London, son of a shopkeeper. Thanks to the patronage of Sir Edward Coke, he was educated at Charterhouse and at Pembroke Hall, Cambridge; for a year he occupied a chaplaincy in the wealthy household of Sir William Masham, fell in love with one of its young ladies but was rejected as unsuitable, and in December 1629 married one of the maids. By this time he had become a Puritan, carrying his rejection of Anglican ceremonial and church government further than most of the party cared publicly to go. In December 1630 he sailed for New England, arriving in Boston on February 5, 1631. Invited to become minister at the church there, he refused because the congregation had not explicitly "separated" from the Church of England; for two years he lived in Plymouth, occasionally preaching but not officially ordained.

Called to the church in Salem in 1633, he rapidly put himself in opposition to the regime of the colony by declaring that the royal charter gave no valid title to the land, denying that a magistrate could tender an oath of civil obedience to the unregenerate, continuing to insist that the churches profess separation, and asserting that the civil authorities should not punish breaches of the first four Commandments. On October 9, 1635, the General Court

of Massachusetts Bay sentenced him to banishment; in
January, warned that the authorities were about to deport
him to England, he fled to the uninhabited regions of the
south, outside the limits of Massachusetts, and in that summer founded the settlement he named Providence.

He lived by farming and by trading with the Indians,
whose language he learned and whose absolute trust he
won; thereby he was able to do heroic service for the
rest of New England in the Pequot War of 1637. In
great part because of him the ultimate battle of extinc-
tion was staved off until King Philip's War of 1675-1676.
As the Narragansett area filled up with a variety of settlers,
most of them refugees from Massachusetts, the communities suffered both from their own intestine rivalries and
from expansionist designs of Massachusetts and Connecticut. Being the foremost citizen, although not with all inhabitants the most popular, Williams was sent in 1643 to
England; there in 1644 he secured from Parliament a
charter uniting the several towns into the colony of Rhode
Island, fixing its boundaries and guaranteeing its independence. He also published three volumes. A leader in
the painful and often desperate effort to organize a government for the colony, he was again sent to London in
November 1651, at a moment when internal dissension
seemed on the point of destroying it. He added to his reputation by publishing three more books, became a friend
of John Milton, conversed with Cromwell and saved his
charter.

For three years, 1654 to 1657, he served as "president"
of the colony, which was essentially being governor, although the disorganization was so great that he never had
anything like control. Thereafter he acted in various pub-

lic capacities, constantly concerned with Indian affairs, and wore himself out, subsiding at last into a venerable but lonely old age. In 1672 he engaged three Quakers in a tumultuous public debate for four long days, and wrote a report on it that was printed at Boston in 1676. Well over seventy, he took part as a soldier as well as a negotiator in Philip's War. In his last years he had to be supported by his son; he died impoverished in the spring of 1683 and was buried with military honors.[1]

was opposed to state + ch relationship
not merely that but there were reasons
why he opposed such. He did not
want loyalty to the state to interfere
with a man's religious beliefs.

a progenitor of separatism

II The Evolution of a Prophet

I

In so far as the Great Migration to Massachusetts Bay in 1630 was inspired by religion—there were of course, for many of the rank and file at least, economic inducements—it was a resolution to obey what to the leaders of this particular segment of the Puritan party seemed a clear commandment of God: to imitate the precise form of church organization described in the New Testament. These people so read the Bible as to make out what we now call a Congregational polity, which demanded two peculiar features. It declared that all churches were "particular," equal in status, and that above them there should exist no hierarchy of ecclesiastical superiors, neither bishops nor presbyteries; this equality and autonomy followed from the fact that each church was founded, at the moment of its incorporation, on an explicit and verbal covenant, publicly sworn to by the members. No one could be a churchman unless he specifically attested a concrete covenant, nor could a man be a minister apart from being so designated by a congregation; there could be no "minister at large," and hence no bishop nor presbytery. Secondly, Congregationalism required that membership be severely limited to the "visible" saints, to those openly examined before the assembled church, who could make a convincing "relation" of their spiritual experience, and who could demonstrate their ability to swear to the covenant.

On these propositions the colonizers differed not only from the established Church of England but, more disastrously, from the vast majority of their Puritan brethren, who were Presbyterians and did not believe that either the church covenant or the restricted membership was prescribed in the New Testament. The leaders of the enterprise were thus a minority within the Puritan movement; they could look ahead and see that even if the Puritans were someday to overthrow the Church of England and step into the place of the bishops, Congregational Puritans would be no better off under a Presbyterian establishment than under an Anglican.

However, save for their divergence on these peculiarities of church polity, the New Englanders had no quarrel whatsoever with the social philosophy of their day; they were entirely at one with both their Presbyterian brethren and their Anglican enemies in believing that in any society only one orthodox regime should be allowed and that the civil magistrate should suppress and, if necessary, extirpate every form of ecclesiastical or doctrinal dissent. They were legitimists, wanting to be law-abiding, conservative; they held it axiomatic that the state should protect the orthodox doctrine and way of life (once the clergy had defined it), punish heresy, and compel all inhabitants, whether church members or not, to attend services and pay taxes for the support of the ministry. They were as little capable of imagining that civil peace might comport with the allowance of religious differences as a capitalist society would be of conceiving that dissident economies may exist within the national system.

As the sign of legitimacy, the colony had a charter, issued in 1629 by King Charles I to the Massachusetts Bay Company; this delegated royal sovereignty to the corporation, thereby empowering it to act as he did in England—to suppress heresy and put subversives to death. As a corresponding sign of legitimacy in their churches, the ministers strenuously advertised that they had never separated from the Church of England. They held that church unhappily tainted by such paraphernalia as bishops and ceremonials, but said that the parish churches were Congregational at the core and therefore "true" churches. The cornerstones of the regime so rapidly and successfully established in Massachusetts were the theology of the covenant and this principle of Nonseparation. Williams was the first, and most conspicuous, to strike at these foundations. Thus he became, as indeed he remains, a menace to society.[1]

In England these Congregational or Independent Puritans had already been acutely embarrassed by groups of the overzealous who reasoned—or rather, compulsively felt—that if a covenanted church should consist only of tried saints, then the parish churches, where everybody in a mere geographical area was regarded as a member, were hopelessly corrupt and should be denounced. They took the awful step of becoming "Separatists." (One such group, harried out of England in 1609, had, in 1620, washed up at Plymouth, where the survivors were trying to live down their past by behaving in as orthodox a fashion as their meager resources allowed.) These radicals were in no sense believers in religious liberty; they simply could not put up, even temporarily, with the established order. They were naturally regarded with horror by the authorities, but with even more loathing by the Puritans, because they justified the authorities' charge that Puritanism led to sedition, and with the utmost hatred by Congregational Puritans, because they used Congregational polity as an excuse for their rebellion. The civil and religious chiefs of the Massachusetts experiment were on the alert to detect and stamp out the slightest stirring of the Separatist spirit. Otherwise they would be convicted, in their own eyes no less than in the eyes of the world, of being an illegitimate and treasonable conspiracy, incapable of enforcing a civilized discipline.

Roger Williams was known among the fraternity in Essex to have exceptionally violent antipathies to the Book of Common Prayer and to Anglican ceremonial; it seems that there were already fears that he had embarked on the fatal descent into Separatism. These suspicions he confirmed, showing that he had indeed gone over the brink by refusing to accept the call of Boston because the people were not confessed Separatists. (That he, despite the rumors, should be offered the post shows how great was his reputation for scholarship and piety.[2]) All his trouble at Salem from 1633 to 1635— the political heresies he there devised—were consequences of his effort to impose Separatism on Massachusetts or, failing that, to force Salem to separate from the rest of Massachusetts.

Out of this premise came his argument that the King of England had no title to the land of the Indians and so no right to issue a charter; wherefore, the colony had no warrant to enforce conformity to Nonseparation. Likewise, a people who officially believed in regenerate membership could not logically treat the unregenerate as capable of

swearing to and obeying an oath; wherefore the regime
had no warrant to enforce loyalty on the masses. Because
he did thus threaten the very bases of the society, at a
moment when the possibility of an Anglican invasion to
recover the charter and to reduce Massachusetts to conformity with England was real, the state dealt with him
as any state must deal with such agitators. The statesmen
who exiled him never repented.

Yet now, as all the world knows, this Separatist figures in
history as the pioneer of religious freedom, even of democracy. In the monumentally sculptured pantheon of inter-
national Protestantism at Geneva, where Gustavus Adol-
phus represents Sweden and Oliver Cromwell stands for
England, the American delegate is neither Winthrop nor
Cotton, but Williams. Some even hail him as the precursor
of Jefferson, of liberalism and of rationalism; they call him
the prophet of the splendid doctrine that a man's right to
worship as he pleases is inalienably given him by nature
and nature's God.

His contemporaries would be utterly bewildered by this
estimate, especially those who knew why they got rid of
him. To them, Williams was a recognizable—and tedious—
type: one who took the Bible with a foolish literalness. The
only mystery was how a scholar of his intelligence, warmth
and charm could fall into this sort of pedantry, which generally flourished among boors lacking all sense of perspec-
tive. He refused to admit either his own fallibility or the
practical considerations of a long-range policy; he went
off half-cocked; he turned complex and subtle ideals into
slapdash slogans. He was the worst kind of virtuous man,
a perfectionist who made dogmas out of purity and demanded that the rest of the world conform to him rather

than he to them. Roger Williams was exiled as much because he was a nuisance as because he was subversive.

It is indeed a shame that the image with which posterity has replaced the Williams whom Governor John Winthrop sent into exile bears so little relation to the fascinating reality. Winthrop, Bradford and several who opposed him felt for him an irresistible affection. A serious disservice has been done to the liberal, the Protestant, the patriotic traditions of this country by well-meaning panegyrists who, in making Williams over into their own terms, have made him unavailable to a day which has need of him. The reader of this volume will, I hope, have in his hands enough of Williams' own words to comprehend him for what he was, with all his crotchets and his magnificence, and to realize that he offers justifications for freedom which may prove more pertinent to our necessities than many of the eighteenth and nineteenth-century formulas that have tragically crumbled before our very eyes.

II

No one of those who sought his destruction—not even his archenemy, the Reverend John Cotton—would have insulted Williams by saying, as does a modern encomium: "The cast of his thought was social rather than theological." Even for theologians in an ultratheological era, the cast of Williams' mind was much too theological: therein consists his challenge to the twentieth century as well as to the seventeenth.

He came, let me repeat, to his final positions because he began as a Separatist, because he was driven by religious

passion, not because he was mollified by the religious indif-
ferentism of a Jefferson. He preached liberty of conscience
not because he thought it the least destructive or most
economical way for men to live together, but because of a
vision which for him was a never-ending ecstasy. He did
not look forward to a free society as the goal of human
endeavor; instead, he looked down on it, in pity and sorrow, seeing in freedom only a preliminary requirement for
the Christian pilgrimage. He remained to the end a stal-
wart Calvinist, believing firmly in predestination, reproba-
tion, irresistible grace and, above all, in perseverance of
the saints. Hence his rage against the Quakers. The quirk
that distinguishes Williams from a Winthrop or a Cotton
was simply that he took these doctrines of Calvinism with
such utter consistency that rather than settle for a rough
approximation to the kingdom of God on earth, he demanded the real thing or nothing at all. The cast of his
mind was not social: it was so exclusively religious that to
him the doctrine of the covenant as propounded in orthodox New England seemed a prostitution of theology to
social expediency.

Therefore, only as a footnote to his major theme did he
begin in 1631 by saying that magistrates should not enforce
the duties of the "First Table"—the first four of the Ten
Commandments, which pertain to the private spiritual
life—and that their concern with the "Second Table"
should be limited to matters like theft and adultery, which
have social consequences. Winthrop and the authorities
were not sympathetic, but for a while were not too much
disturbed by this aberration; what worried them about
Williams was his Separatism. His objections to the com-
pulsive role of government became dangerous only after

he made clear that they were linked with his effort to push Massachusetts into separation. And only after he was exiled, had suffered the snows and the hunger, only after he had learned what it meant to try to rule the explosive spirits who followed him or who trooped uninvited into his colony—only then could he think his way out of his original premise, only then recognize that what had been his minor theme had become his major. At the end of his course, he perceived that the problem for a man who wishes to guard his independence in society is how he should spiritually separate not from this or that abuse, but from society itself.

He never intended, when forbidding magistrates to enforce the First Table, to put natural right ahead of the Holy Spirit. On the contrary, he wanted to keep the state from so commanding the Christian that his endeavor for perfection would not be contaminated by social approbation. He who tries to believe as a duty of citizenship is fatally clogged. Hence, although Williams is celebrated as the prophet of religious freedom, he actually exerted little or no influence on institutional developments in America; only after the conception of liberty for all denominations had triumphed on wholly other grounds did Americans look back on Williams and invest him with his ill-fitting halo. For him there was never any virtue in freedom of and by itself; freedom was something negative, which protects men from worldly compulsions in a world where any compulsion, most of all one to virtue, increases the quantity of sin. Liberty was a way of not adding to the stock of human depravity; were men not sinful, there would be no need of freedom. When we call him a "prophet," we vulgarize the word to mean one who fore-

tells, a prognosticator. But Williams was a prophet in
the Old Testament sense, one who demands that the world
listen to what the Lord Jehovah speaks through his lips.
Like an Isaiah or a Jeremiah, he found himself at war with
his fellow citizens because he pronounced judgment on
what they thought was a good and righteous community.
So his contemporaries could recognize his disease: it was
a delusion of grandeur. Where did he get the authority
for his arrogance? At best he was insane; at the worst,
conceited. They could not help liking him, but they
wearied of his self-pity, his cloudiness, his incessant haggling over minutiae. A great many found him not so much
dangerous as merely exasperating.

All this appears in the comments of those who either
knew him or knew about him. Bradford was a judicious
and humane man; he called Williams godly and zealous,
confessing that he himself benefited from Williams' ad-
monitions—although he insinuated that these exhortations
did not always seem to agree with Scripture. Bradford
held him merely unsettled in judgment, and so more to be
pitied and prayed for than condemned.[3] For years after
the exile, Winthrop corresponded warmly with Williams—
Winthrop's letters are lost, but Williams' replies show the
tone—and broke off the interchange only when Williams
showed that despite respect and affection he would fight
for Rhode Island's territory against Massachusetts' aggres-
sion.[4] Yet Williams' relations with the son of this governor,
John Winthrop the younger, who for years was the foremost citizen of Connecticut and, after the charter of 1662
until his death in 1676, its governor, were those of genuine
comradeship: "Your loving lines in this cold, dead season," Williams wrote him in February 1660, "were as a

cup of your Connecticut cider, which we are glad to hear abounds with you, or of that western metheglin, which you and I have drunk at Bristol together"—a reference to December 1630 when the two young men had started for America together.[5]

Thus his contemporaries saw him as a man of ability unfortunately spoiled by eccentricity. As this opinion hardened into settled conviction, we perceive that by the end of the century it had become a way of smothering his ideas. In 1680, when the battered Williams was still alive, William Hubbard composed, at the order of the General Court, a history of New England; Hubbard was a moderate and a relatively tolerant character, but he described Williams' gyrations as no more than a case of overheated zeal, remembering that even back in Essex Williams was reputed to be "divinely mad." By the time Cotton Mather wrote the *Magnalia* (published in 1702), both he and his father Increase had accepted, at least officially, the Revolution of 1689 and the Toleration Act. However, he did not on this account regard Williams as a forerunner; Williams seemed to him no apostle of liberty but simply a frenetic creature.

Mather employed a characteristically Matherian simile— it has been often quoted—of a Dutch windmill so violently turned round in a storm that the stones themselves caught fire; so, he said, was America "like to be set on fire by the rapid motion of a windmill in the head of one particular man." The trouble with Williams was psychological or even physiological: there once was a gentleman who had "an humour of making singular and fanciful expositions of Scripture," but a certain Dr. Sim gave him such a dose of "physick" as made him immediately orthodox. "Pity this

Dr. Sim had but undertaken the cure of our Mr. Williams."[6]

None of this ridicule is addressed to the Williams whom modern liberalism adores; that Williams was so little of a threat he was not worth noting. But the Williams who was divinely mad, who had a "humour," posed more of a problem for an age slowly but inexorably moving toward toleration than did the advocate of freedom. There was something in his methodology, rather than his conclusions, which aroused the real distrust, excited fear. The satires try to conceal this danger, but Mather's clumsy story of Dr. Sim betrays everything: orthodox Protestants were less alarmed by Williams' libertarianism than by the way he read the Bible. He was a maverick among the intellectuals of New England because he interpreted the relation of the Old Testament to the New not as an unfolding through time of an enduring covenant between God and man—a covenant within which men were still living and within which American governments could confidently operate—but as a radical break.

He belonged to that rare and furtive brotherhood who, here and there throughout the centuries, have taken the New Testament to mean not a continuation but a repudiation of the Old. He would be a Christian, but not a Christianized Jew. He believed the Bible from cover to cover, yet he would not read the Old Testament only as a historical document: he expounded it "typologically." Here is the secret of his Separatism and of his divergence from his colleagues (they so feared and detested it that they tried to conceal it). Here is the insight that guided him from his initial separation to his ultimate vision of the predicament of men and nations.

III

Typology is a peculiar method of interpreting the Bible, specifically the relation of the Old Testament to the New, in a way that finds inner, mystical correspondences which make unnecessary and actually irrelevant any concern for the literal, historical facts of Israel's career. The typologist, when you find him at his purest, does not care about dates nor about the social customs of Judea; he insists that events recorded in the Old Testament, including the prophecies, are preformulations of events in the life of Christ, or enunciations of principles which then were dark but the meaning of which Christ made clear. For example: Joseph descended into a pit, and Jonah into the belly of a whale; nobody can read these accounts without feeling that more is intended than the narrators comprehended, but they did not have the key and so simply told their stories. Christ solved the cryptogram: both Joseph and Jonah are "types" of His descent into hell, and Christ is the "antitype."

The chosen people enacted in history a drama they never understood, and many episodes—the drunkenness of Noah, Jacob and his concubines, the incest of Lot—would, if taken only as historical occurrences, be simply filthy. But within this dumb show was hidden a meaning; the Savior reveals to a literal-minded humanity that the Old Testament was a rehearsal to be taken not literally but figuratively. The narrative of Israel, radiating this aura of anticipation, must be translated into the doctrines of Christianity. It is not really an account of kings and harlots, but an allegory. When viewed in this light, the repressive and persecuting actions of Jewish sovereigns are not precedents for modern rulers, but typological pointers toward the methods by which, in the antitype, ministers should pronounce purely spiritual condemnations.

Typology had for centuries been a special subdivision of the allegorical method. It appears to have originated among the Alexandrine Jews in the first century of the Christian era; they, coming into contact with the sophisticated culture of Greece, were ashamed of the barbarity and crudity of their sacred books, but were relieved to discover that the Greeks long since had devised an allegorical method for extracting dignified truths out of the undignified passages of Homer. The method was introduced into Christian exegesis mainly by Origen in the third century, who found in Judaism a "veiled Christianity," and even allegorized the New Testament so that it in turn became no more than an introduction to "an unwritten and spiritual reality." From the beginning, among Jews and Christians, the allegorical method and its child, the typological interpretation, were opposed by practical men.

Typology was constantly accused of being overingenious, a subversion of the plain truths of the Gospel, of being imaginative and capricious. It was denounced as mistaking the subjectivity of overwrought brains for the firm meaning of the Bible. All this weight of Christian tradition was mobilized behind Winthrop and Cotton against what seemed to them the absurdities of Roger Williams.

The weight was especially heavy in the New England societies because these were Protestant communities; the great Protestant reformers had been very explicit in their condemnation of the typological method along with every other variant of the allegorical. Luther and Calvin depended heavily on Augustine, but primarily for support of their doctrines of predestination and divine sovereignty; they disregarded that Augustine who, in his *Confessions*, marked a stage on his road to faith when he heard "one or two places of the Old Testament resolved, and oft times in a figure [*i.e.*, in a metaphor or a type]; which when I understood literally I was slain spiritually." They pretended that Augustine had never devoted pages to proving that the drunkenness of Noah, so unedifying in the literal sense, was "a figure of the death and passion of Christ." The Reformers were the more resolved to expunge this method from Biblical exegesis because they were convinced that in the late Middle Ages (as we call them) the allegorical and typological interpretations had become a riot of irresponsible divinations.

After disciples of Bonaventura had gone so far beyond Thomas Aquinas (who allowed, as he still today allows Thomists, the four levels of meaning—historical, moral, allegorical and analogical) as to formulate an eightfold significance, Luther thought it time to call a halt and to assert: "The literal sense of Scripture alone is the whole essence of faith and of Christian theology." Each passage, Luther declared, has one clear, definite and true sense of its own; allegories are empty speculations, "and as it were the scum of Holy Scripture." He called allegory and the scheme of types a "harlot" seducing "idle" men. Calvin was, if anything, more emphatic. "It is better," he said, "to confess ignorance than to play with frivolous guesses." The English Reformers, herein exhibiting perhaps their English temperament, were furiously hostile to all typological speculations. Tyndale, for example, in *The Obedi-*

ence of a Christian Man, said in 1528: "Such allegory
proveth nothing, it is a mere simile. God is a Spirit, and
all His words are spiritual, and His literal sense is spiritual." In the early seventeenth century, during all the bitter struggle for power between Puritans and Anglicans,
both sides agreed at least on this, that a drawing of mystic
meanings from the Bible was something with which men
were not to be trusted.

Thus we may define Roger Williams as a man who
trusted himself, trusted his reading and his insight, and
was prepared to pay the price. How he came to embrace
this heresy is something of a mystery, but the lines of his
development are moderately clear. In most typological
theory, as in Augustine's, the emphasis had been on the
continuity rather than on the dislocation between the two
Testaments; it endeavored to decipher a universal reign of
Christian rationality by which even the most intemperate
of the Jews had—unconsciously to be sure—been governed.
In rage or in lust, Saul, David and Solomon had done
things which, repeated within the altered framework of
the risen Messiah, yielded up new instead of the hitherto
baffling, not to say seductive, meanings. Typologists so
strained their ingenuity to find mystical significances in
Kings and Chronicles that they confirmed such forthright
men as Jerome, Luther and Calvin in their conviction that
the whole inquiry was both fantastic and dangerous.

Because English Puritans did read the Bible in a Protestant spirit, they found in it the description of the primitive
church, and so tried to reduce the Church of England to
conformity with this fact. Presbyterians, it is true, found
the Apostles setting up Presbyterian churches, while the

Independents interpreted them as Congregationalists; yet these differences, important as they might be, were differences of fact, not of poetic imagery.

In the same spirit, Puritan theologians—especially those who came to New England—read about the covenant which God had established with Abraham, and so organized their churches on a covenant among the saints which included their "seed." By this sort of reading, they produced a theology, an ecclesiastical program, and a social philosophy for New England. They did not entirely condemn typology; the founders of New England recognized that it, if used with extreme caution, might have its uses. John Cotton experimented with it to the very limits of safety (for that reason Williams and he were bound to become enemies), but almost to a man the New England theologians, especially such vigorous leaders as Thomas Hooker and Peter Bulkeley, were so content with the consistency of their covenant or "federal" version of the Bible that they saw in typology only a fantastic creation of the imagination which had no place in sound scholarship or in orthodox society.

Most typologists had, as I say, aimed at proving a continuity between the Testaments, at showing that a steady, unalterable scheme of law had reigned from Adam to the Apostles. But the danger always was not only that typologists might torture the Old Testament to yield up private fancies, but that, in their eagerness to make the New Testament pertain to a different order of intelligibility, they would make the division between the Testaments a chasm. If the kings of Israel were types of Christ, then they were not examples of pious conduct for modern sovereigns, and their executions of heretics and witches were no models for New England magistrates. The horror in that prospect was obvious: where then would the magistrates get any guidance to righteous political conduct?

Williams certainly formulated the logic of typology in an especially sharp, or one might even say brutal, fashion; perhaps it was because in order to become a Puritan at all he had to make the violent gesture of coming out, of separating; or possibly it was just that he had a violent imagination. At any rate, his immense distinction is that, involved with the Massachusetts oligarchy over the question of whether they should or should not declare themselves Separatists, he was forced to go farther than he had intended, and so to maintain the utter impossibility of New England's magistrates, or of any other rulers or sachems in the world, being antitypes of Israel's sovereigns. The more earnestly they imitated Jewish governors, the more he was obliged to accuse them of becoming traitors to the Christian dispensation. Further meditation on the reasons which brought him to this point—in the solitude of the wilderness, amid savages and hard work—at last emboldened him to say that no modern community any longer possesses in the physical realm those sanctions with which Israel alone had been invested. Therefore the modern magistrate must get along as best he can, trying to do no more than keep the peace, while the authentic antitypes of Old Testament heroes spend their lives in this pilgrimage searching for that church which Christ destroyed and for which no earthly counterpart can any longer exist.

On this basis—and on this basis alone—Roger Williams became the prophet of religious liberty in America.

IV

Governor John Winthrop was a lawyer who thought in terms of history (his *Journal,* which he kept in order to write out of it, he hoped, such a history as Bradford later achieved for Plymouth, shows how to his comprehension events fell out in seemingly illogical sequences, leaving man to find the design in the carpet, and not to cast them arbitrarily into rubrics given *a priori* by typology); as far as such a man could—or can—be, he was magnanimous. In January 1634 he wrote to John Endecott, of Salem, who hitherto had been a loyal if a somewhat impetuous soldier of orthodoxy, but who at that moment seemed seduced by the much more impetuous arguments of Williams against the charter. Winthrop had read Williams' manuscript treatise (it is lost to posterity, undoubtedly destroyed by the government), but he was not impressed. If Williams, he said, "allow not allegories, he must condemn his own writings and speeches, seeing no man useth them more than himself: and this very treatise of his exceeds all that ever I have read (of so serious an argument) in figures and flourishes."

Deep in Williams' being lay this aptitude for figures and allegories; nothing for him was more congenial, as nothing was more antipathetic to Winthrop, than to conceive of historical Israel as an allegory of a church which exists not on land or sea. Winthrop might be compared to—he was more generous than—a modern man of affairs, brought up on Longfellow, when confronted with T. S. Eliot or Kafka.

As for Williams, being a rhetorician of allegory, he could not bear to see Charles I or Governor Winthrop take unto themselves those accouterments of power which Christ had turned into metaphors.

Winthrop was a modest man, but he saw in himself another Joshua: he asked Endecott to compare the one history with the other. Even Williams would have to admit that before the settlement of Massachusetts, God Himself had wiped out the Indians by a plague; this was not a fact to be ignored according to the scheme of cause and effect which constitutes history rather than poetry. Was it not within the same dimension of divine providence as were similar interventions in the Old Testament? "If we had no right to this land, yet our God hath right to it, and if He be pleased to give it us (taking it from a people who had so long usurped upon him, and abused His creatures), who shall control Him or His terms?" If you have to deal with the concrete facts of America just as they come up, one by one, and thereafter a providential design appears among them leading to success, why should this pattern be condemned simply because it happens to resemble the sort of favor shown by the same Jehovah to the chosen people of old? Why condemn it in the name of some other standard, some fanciful construct of an allegory? Why hesitate to regard yourself as chosen?

In 1636 Winthrop was consoled to received from a reliable English correspondent, who had known Williams before 1630, an assurance that Williams was "passionate and precipitate." He was even more reassured in 1637, in the midst of the agony of the Anne Hutchinson crisis, to hear from an anonymous friend an account of the gossip in Puritan circles accusing New England of Separatism, which complimented him to this extent: "Your disclaiming of Mr. Williams' opinions and your dealing with him so as we hear you did, took off much prejudice from you with us, and hath stopped the mouths of some." Winthrop was cautious—after all, who could tell, there might be something in this allegorizing—but in May 1637, when he defended an order of the General Court permitting the authorities to expel undesirables (that is, those whom the magistrates thought sympathetic to Anne Hutchinson), oddly enough he struck not at Anne's Antinomians but at his friend Williams:

Admit a true Christian should come over, and should maintain community of goods, or that magistrates ought not to punish the breakers of the First Table or the members of churches for criminal offences, or that no man were bound to be subject to those laws or magistrates to which they should not give an explicit consent: I hope no man will say that not to receive such an one were to reject Christ. For such opinions (though being maintained in simple ignorance, they might stand with a state of grace, yet) they may be so dangerous to the public weal in many respects, as it would be our sin and unfaithfulness to receive such among us, except it were for trial of their reformation.

Williams might dazzle him with ingenious readings of the Bible, but a hard-pressed executive like Winthrop knew what could be tolerated and what could not in a society for which he was responsible.

Meanwhile he was getting reports from the exile about Indian maneuvers in the Pequot country, which were superb pieces of military intelligence. But along with them came more and more weird preachments. The Pequots may

have committed murder, but still they were not compara-
ble to the servants who slew King Joash, for he was a "type
of Jesus." Just how the head of a state at war was to distinguish between ordinary murderers and those who had
slain a type of Jesus remained obscure to John Winthrop.
He was hardly enlightened in July 1637, when he received
a thirty-seven-page treatise from Providence (it too has
perished) on "the differences between Israel and all other
states." But he could hardly miss the point of the admonition accompanying the discourse, and certainly could not
be expected, when thus addressed, to accept the consequences of such a distinction between type and antitype:

I know, and am persuaded that your misguidings are
great and lamentable, and the further you pass in your
way, the further you wander, and have the further to come
back; and the end of one vexation will be but the beginning of another, till conscience be permitted (though erroneous) to be free amongst you.

We may indeed feel that Winthrop was tried beyond
the limits of charity, when, just as victory was being won
and the heathen were being either slaughtered or taken
in gratifying numbers—exactly as enemies of the Israelites
fared in the Old Testament—he should receive a plea from
Williams for mercy toward the captives: "Sir, concerning
captives (pardon my wonted boldness), the Scripture is
full of mystery, and the Old Testament of types."

Clearly the man had gone mad, like all megalomaniacs,
meditating on only one subject. The wisdom of sober
Christianity, especially of Protestantism, had always
warned that in typology such madness lay. This typologist

justified suspicion by coming up, out of all his hardship, with a blanket pronouncement that even erroneous consciences should be tolerated in civilized society and savage prisoners ought to be set free!

V

Only a few letters survive out of Williams' writings during the years of his controversy with Massachusetts (although, as we have seen, he wrote at least two tracts); so we have to make out his development from guarded entries in Winthrop's *Journal,* or from Williams' later and highly colored reminiscences (see pages 228-229, 237-239). But the best evidences of what happened to his mind are the great publications of 1644.

He reached Boston in 1631 persuaded that truly reformed churches ought to separate and magistrates should not spoil the first four Commandments by enforcing them. That he should hold these positions out of nothing more than a too-eager Puritanism was comprehensible to those who disagreed with him, who had dealt with similar extremists (as they had dealt with John Endecott) and brought them back to sanity. But instead of yielding to the logic of Winthrop and of demonstrable history—instead of seeing what clearly was to be seen by the most recent arrival in America: that this state was a covenanted people and therefore a reproduction in the wilderness of sanctified Israel—Williams alone among the settlers persisted in saying that such patriotism was based on a misreading of the Bible. (Anne Hutchinson and her Antinomians never

came anywhere near this idea.) Why Williams thus stood
out may be translated, though at great risk, into some such
modern equivalent as a principle of literary criticism.

The deeper he progressed into the structure of allegory
and metaphor, the more he found the Old Testament a
prophetic rather than a factual book. But the more he understood that it was not to be taken literally, the more he
estranged himself from the historical mentality that proposed to govern Massachusetts and Connecticut in Israel's
image. The orthodox accused him of an inability to read
the Bible in the light of circumstances and conditions—
they said he imposed on it meanings invented by himself;
he became thereby the more convinced that they, in an
eagerness to accommodate allegory to their self-interest,
had lost the meaning of Christianity.

By the time the score was added up, and Williams had
endured the winter of flight—by the time he had become
the indispensable intermediary between his antagonists and
the heathen fury—he found out why he had first preached
Separatism: the nation of Israel had never, in historical
fact, been such a model of charity as Winthrop expected
to create in America. It had never been anything more
than a type, imperfect and physical, of an ideal which was
as unattainable in America as in Europe. Wherefore, governments which, like that of Massachusetts, pretended to
follow the example of Israel, were behind the times. (Williams might have said, but did not, that it was as though a
prince should try to imitate Hamlet, not realizing that
Hamlet is a literary creation.) Persecution of dissidents, in
communities possessing no other guidance than the cal-
culus of sinful nature, was no way to become the antitype.
A break had occurred in history; the model was no model;

only the sword of the spirit should any longer have real effect. Mere governments had better allow as much freedom as possible.

Governor Winthrop was uneasy in his mind about the banishment of Williams, and in October 1636 sent him a series of inquiries, asking what Williams now, on second thought, imagined he had gained by his folly, whether he believed that the Lord had forsaken New England (that Winthrop should want the opinion of a typologist on this historical question is indeed remarkable), and finally posed the essential question: "From what spirit and to what end do you drive?"

Williams' answer, on October 24, is not full nor entirely candid. He was saving up his thoughts on typology, trying to make sense out of them even while he was receiving the chastening impact of life among savages. But speaking as a Separatist who now was well on his way into the heart of typology, and who certainly was resolved, if ever the time or opportunity came, to speak out, he thus tentatively replied to the Governor of Massachusetts Bay.

Letter to Governor John Winthrop, October 24, 1636

> Providence the 24th of the 8th
> [October 24, 1636]

Sir, Worthy and Wellbeloved:

I WAS abroad about the Pequot business when your letter arrived, and since messengers have fitted, &c.

I therefore now thankfully acknowledge your wisdom and gentleness in receiving so lovingly my late rude and foolish lines: you bear with fools gladly because you are wise.

I still wait upon your love and faithfulness for those poor papers, and cannot but believe that your heart, tongue, and pen should be one, if I were Turk or Jew. . . .

Your first query then is this:

"What have you gained by your new-found practices?"

I confess my gains cast up in man's exchange are loss of friends, esteem, maintenance; but what was gain in that respect I desire to count loss for the excellency of the knowledge of Christ Jesus my Lord. To His all glorious name I know I have gained the honor of one of His poor witnesses, though in sackcloth.

To your beloved selves, and others of God's people yet asleep, this witness in the Lord's season at your waking shall be prosperous; and the seed sown shall arise to the greater purity of the kingdom and ordinances of the Prince of the kings of the earth. . . .

To your second, *viz.*, "Is your spirit as even as it was seven years since?"

I will not follow the fashion, either in commending or condemning of myself. You and I stand at one dreadful, dreadful tribunal: yet what is past I desire to forget, and to press forward towards the mark for the price of the high calling of God in Christ.

And for the evenness of my spirit: Toward the Lord I hope I more long to know and do His holy pleasure only; and to be ready not only to be banished but to die in New England for the name of the Lord Jesus. . . .

To your third, *viz.*, "Are you not grieved that you have grieved so many?"

I say with Paul, I vehemently sorrow for the sorrow of any of Zion's daughters, who should ever rejoice in her king. Yet I must (and O that I had not cause!) grieve because so many of Zion's daughters see not and grieve not for their souls' defilements, and that so few bear John company in weeping after the unfolding of the seals, which only weepers are acquainted with. . . .

Sir, you request me to be free with you, and therefore blame me not if I answer your request, desiring the like payment from your own dear hand, at any time, in any thing.

And let me add that amongst all the people of God— wheresoever scattered about Babel's banks, either in Rome or England—your case is the worst by far: because while others of God's Israel tenderly respect such as desire to fear the Lord, your very judgment and conscience leads you to smite and beat your fellow servants, expel them your coasts, and therefore—though I know the elect shall never be forsaken—yet Sodom's, Egypt's, Amalek's, Babel's judgments ought to drive us out, to make our calling out of this world to Christ, and our election sure in Him.

Sir, your fifth is: "From what spirit, and to what end do you drive?"

Concerning my spirit, as I said before, I could declaim against it; but whether the spirit of Christ Jesus, for whose visible kingdom and ordinances I witness, or the spirit of Antichrist against whom only I contest, do drive me, let the Father of spirits be pleased to search. And (worthy Sir) be you also pleased by the Word to search: and I hope you will find that, as you say you do, I also seek Jesus who was nailed to the gallows, I ask the way to lost Zion, I witness what I believe I see patiently (the Lord assisting) in sackcloth, I long for the bright appearance of the Lord Jesus to consume the man of sin, I long for the appearance of the Lamb's wife, also New Jerusalem. I wish heartily prosperity to you all, governor and people, in your civil way, and mourn that you see not your poverty, nakedness, in spirituals. And yet I rejoice in the hopes that as the way of the Lord to Apollo, so within a few years (through, I fear though, many tribulations) the way of the Lord Jesus, the first and most ancient path, shall be more plainly discovered to you and me. . . .

But while another judgeth the condition fair, the soul that fears, doubts, and feels a guilt, hath broken bones. Now, worthy Sir, I must call up your wisdom, your love, your patience, your promise and faithfulness, candid ingenuity. My heart's desire is abundant, and exceeds my pen. . . . Where I err, Christ be pleased to restore me; where I stand, to establish. If you please, I have also a few queries to yourself; without your leave, I will not, but will ever mourn (the Lord assisting) that I am no more (though I hope ever) yours,

Roger Williams

III Prophet in a Wilderness

I

SCOTTISH PRESBYTERIANS were to a man completely hostile to every idea Williams entertained, but they expended most of their venom (which was considerable) on their fellow Puritans, the English Independents (who blocked their march to power) and on New England Congregationalists. One of their foremost spokesmen, Robert Baillie, sneered in 1645 that Williams' proposals would subject king and parliaments "to the free will of the promiscuous multitude," but oddly enough this dour Baillie seems to have known and liked Roger Williams. In the same blast he also sneered at orthodox New England for making no progress in the conversion of Indians, the aim it had once flaunted in order to win royal favor. "I have read of none of them that seem to have minded this matter: only Williams in the time of his banishment from among them did essay what could be done with those desolate souls, and by a little experience quickly did find a wonderful great facility to gain thousands of them."

Actually, Baillie was as little capable of understanding his strange friend as John Cotton himself. Williams was not a great converter of Indians; in fact, he hardly tried. Not that he doubted his success; on the contrary, he knew how well he could succeed, and endeavored to explain all this to Baillie, who at least printed his statement:

For our New England parts, I can speak it confidently, I know it to have been easy for myself, long ere this, to have brought many thousands of these natives, yea, the whole country to a far greater antichristian conversion than ever was heard of in America. I could have brought the whole country to have observed one day in seven: I add, to have received baptism, to have come to a stated church meeting, to have maintained priests and forms of prayer, and a whole form of antichristian worship, in life and death.

But, he insisted, it would be woe to him "if I call that conversion to God which is indeed the subversion of the souls of millions in Christendom, from one false worship to another." What would be the worth of a Sabbath observance which the simple savages would do out of respect for Williams and not out of conviction (see page 69)? God's method was to turn the soul from its idols before making it capable of worship, and until God had wrought, Williams would no longer, after Massachusetts expelled him, presume to work in God's place.

Williams began to study Indian languages at Plymouth, lodging "with them in their filthy, smoky holes . . . to gain their tongue." Now in the Narragansett wilderness he lived close to them, and for periods at a time with them. He struggled constantly, often in vain, to persuade the orthodox that strict justice to savages would prove in the long run the best policy:

Private interests, both with Indians and English are many; yet these things you may and must do: First, kiss truth where you evidently, upon your soul, see it. 2. Advance justice, though upon a child's eye. 3. Seek and make peace, if possible, with all men. 4. Secure your own life from a revengeful, malicious arrow or hatchet. I have been in danger of them, and delivered yet from them; blessed be His holy name.

Yet never did he sentimentalize the Indians. They were too often "barbarous men of blood, who are as justly to be repelled and subdued as wolves that assault the sheep." (This, we should note, was well after the figure of "the noble savage" had become a stock character in European literature.) Yet he found that because he dealt honestly with them, they trusted him as much as they trusted anybody, and some of them proved stanch friends. He purchased his land from the Indians, and only thereafter sought a charter in London as a protection not against them but against his rapacious English neighbors. He was later to quiet one of the worst contentions among his own people by telling them: "It was not price nor money that could have purchased Rhode Island. Rhode Island was purchased by love"—by the friendship he had won from the sachem of the Narragansett, that Miantonomu whose brutal and cowardly murder the sanctified Commissioners of the United Colonies contrived in 1643 while Williams was away in London.

We marvel how Williams, London-bred and Cambridge-trained, a scholar, linguist and dreamer, learned enough of woodcraft to carry him through the terrible hazards of his occupation. The mass of English settlers showed no aptitude for frontier scouting, and only after a generation had grown up in America were Puritans able to match Philip's braves in forest cunning. That Williams did survive, let alone that to a degree he prospered, proves that he could

and did learn from the Indians. But this fact is not to be ex-
plained solely because of his character, generous and
imaginative as he was: it is more properly a consequence
of his peculiar theology, of that same typological conception of history which made him also a Separatist and ultimately a churchless man seeking the pure fellowship.
Because Christ had abrogated the covenant, Williams
could treat Indian culture with respect. He was the only
Englishman in his generation who could do so.

Nevertheless, his initiation into the wilderness was an
ordeal. No other New England writer makes quite so
much of an incantation out of the very word "wilderness,"
and none of the others who also endured great hardships
so loves to expatiate on them. How he enjoyed feeling
sorry for himself he made evident to the daughter of his
old patron, to the disgust of this Mrs. Sadleir:

In my poor span of time, I have been oft in the jaws of
death, sickening at sea, shipwrecked on shore, in danger of
arrows, swords and bullets: and yet methinks, the most
high and most holy God hath reserved me for some service
to His most glorious and eternal majesty.

He suffered tortures that winter of flight, but he never
thereafter let anybody forget them (see page 229). The
experience deepened his pessimism about this life, and his
letters abound with longings for "the Alpha and Omega of
all blessedness," for escape from the body of this death,
where men are but "poor grasshoppers, hopping and skip-
ping from branch to twig in this vale of tears." Yet despite
this "otherworldliness" and his eagerness for death or for
the end of the world, he fastened his attention on the gram-

mar, the thoughts, the customs, the artifacts of his barbaric associates; on the long voyage to England in 1643 he threw together his notes and his memories to compose *A Key into the Language of America,* which, published shortly after his arrival in London, made him famous as the first literate Englishman who had lived intimately with the Indians, and which would be enough, even had he written no more, to keep his name alive today. It is, indeed, the nearest approach to an objective, anthropological study that anyone was to achieve in America for a century or more.

The secret of the book is—what the modern mind can hardly comprehend—typology. Williams was anything but a social scientist; he was a strict Calvinist who strayed into dangerous allegories. Actually, the theology and polity of orthodox New England were not evangelical in character. The New England Way, as it was called, envisaged a static society, within each unit of which would be the church, sitting tight on its covenant and guarding the gates against promiscuous admission. It conceived the whole community as in covenant with the Absolute, mainly occupied in congratulating itself for not being as others, or else in bewailing the many sins by which it fell short of its obligation. John Eliot became renowned for converting a few Indians in Natick, and the colony made much of him in England in order to answer critics like Baillie; but the theology of the covenant inevitably bred a contempt for lesser breeds outside the covenant, and no federal theologian, not even Eliot, could have treated the Indian way of life courteously enough to have written the *Key.*

But Williams could do it because he believed that in all human history there had been only one nation in covenant with Jehovah, only one chosen people, and that this unique federation had vanished from earth on the morning of Christ's resurrection. From then until the end of the world, nations are no more than civil contrivances for getting along with a minimum of law and order. No country as a country—least of all New England—has a divine blessing peculiar unto itself, and consequently none can exercise such spiritual power in political affairs as did Israel. Thus Narragansett and Mohegan are intrinsically no worse than French or English. There might be more "civility" in Europe, but such amenities are relative. As soon as the uniquely typical and visible state was translated into its antitype, which is the invisible church, all nations were left with no better guides than considerations of utility, prosperity, power or peace. And since humanity is depraved, these guides naturally lead to war, rapine, tyranny. The history of Europe is understandably one of blood and horror, but the history of the New England Indians is not much different or more contemptible. Civilization is not essentially superior to barbarism. Typology relieved Williams of the necessity for being what his covenanted brethren so frequently were, racial or religious snobs.

The book is, in structure, simply a dictionary. The terms are arranged not alphabetically but under thirty-two headings, such as eating, parts of the body, winds, sea, government, trading, war, death. In parallel columns he lists his spelling of the Indian word or phrase, and opposite it his translation. But what gives the book its charm is the fact that whenever a translation starts a train of reflection or associates itself with some unforgettable experience in the wilderness, he lets himself go with an "observation." At the end of each chapter he composes a little meditation on the subject, which he calls a "general observation," and follows it by a verse entitled "More Particular." He was too turgid a writer to submit to the discipline of poetry, and his rhymes are not memorable art; but some of them, which I cannot resist quoting, are ingenious applications of typological doctrine to social philosophy.

The fact that the book has no formal continuity, that it consists merely of a list of words and phrases punctuated by seemingly random observations, has prevented it from being studied by any but anthropologists (who certify its scientific reliability). Most students miss the point of Williams' "directions for use of the language," in which he says that he purposely intended something more than a dictionary "as not so accommodate to the benefit of all." He was hoping that others might also move as fellow citizens among the savages! But most revealing is the prefatory statement that at first he tried to present the material in a "dialogue"—he dearly loved the dramatic—but gave up the idea for the sake of brevity. Nevertheless he says, he so framed each chapter that "I may call it an implicit dialogue." To keep this extract as far as possible faithful to Williams' intention, I have given one full section (from pages eight and nine of the original) of his dialogue, as a fair sample of what lies between his several "observations." One such sample is sufficient; otherwise I have introduced the entry by putting in italics the starting point or the chapter title, to which the observation serves as response in this ingenious (and typological) "implicit" dialogue.

These make clear another trait of Williams' mentality: his penchant for beholding in objects "emblems" of spir-

itual truths. To this mannerism Winthrop objected when
he said that Williams' tract was full of figures and flourishes. It is actually an almost inescapable consequence of
the typological method; he who once begins perceiving in
the Old Testament not factual narratives but ingenious
puzzles to be deciphered only in an imaginative realm outside history is bound also to find things or happenings
around him lose their solidity and dissolve into inward
communications. This emblemizing disposition is utterly
different from the normal Puritan method of reading sermons in stones; theologians of the covenant studied events
(exactly as did Winthrop and Bradford in their histories)
in order to perceive the governing will of God at work.
But they did not find in stone or beast an enigmatic symbol of a divine utterance, and they did not—as still today
their successors do not—approve of the sort of people
who do.

Perhaps it explains the sneaking esteem for Williams
which Cotton Mather could not keep out of his satire: at
a time when Mather was seeking reinforcement for a piety
which the covenant alone could no longer excite, when he
was experimenting with novel ways of "spiritualizing" the
commonplaces of existence, he let himself praise the *Key*
because it "spiritualizes the curiosities." We do not know
whether Edward Taylor was aware of the *Key*, but he in-
dulged his emblemizing as a secret vice and publicly remained loyal to the covenant. The next great figure after
Williams in the line of descent is Jonathan Edwards, who
also rejected the covenant doctrine and constantly brooded
over the meaning of created objects when regarded as
images or shadows or divine things.[1]

A Key into the Language of America: Or, An help to the Language of the Natives in that part of America, called New-England

By Roger Williams of Providence in New-England
London, 1643

To my dear and wellbeloved friends and countrymen, in old and New England:

I PRESENT you with a *Key;* I have not heard of the like, yet framed, since it pleased God to bring that mighty continent of America to light. Others of my countrymen have often and excellently and lately written of the country (and none that I know beyond the goodness and worth of it).

This *Key* respects the native language of it, and happily may unlock some rarities concerning the natives themselves not yet discovered.

I drew the materials in a rude lump at sea, as a private help to my own memory, that I might not by my present absence lightly lose what I had so dearly bought in some few years' hardship and charges among the barbarians; yet being reminded by some what pity it were to bury those materials in my grave at land or sea, and withal remembering how oft I have been importuned by worthy friends of all sorts to afford them some helps this way, I resolved (by the assistance of the most high) to cast those materials into this *Key,* pleasant and profitable for all, but especially for my friends residing in those parts.

A little *Key* may open a box, where lies a bunch of keys.

With this I have entered into the secrets of those countries, wherever English dwell, about two hundred miles between the French and Dutch plantations. For want of this, I know what gross mistakes myself and others have run into. . . .

It is expected that, having had so much converse with these natives, I should write some little of them. . . .

From Adam and Noah that they spring, it is granted on all hands.

But as for their later descent, and whence they came into these parts, it seems as hard to find as to find the wellhead of some fresh stream which, running many miles out of the country to the salt ocean, hath met with many mixing streams by the way. They say themselves that they have sprung and grown up in that very place, like the very trees of the wilderness.

They say that their great God Cawtantowwit created those parts. They have no clothes, books, nor letters, and conceive their fathers never had; and therefore they are easily persuaded that the God that made Englishmen is a greater God because He hath so richly endowed the English above themselves. But when they hear that about sixteen hundred years ago, England and the inhabitants thereof were like themselves, and since have received from God clothes, books, &c., they are greatly affected with a secret hope concerning themselves. . . .

They have many strange relations of one Wetucks, a man that wrought great miracles amongst them, and walking upon the waters, &c., with some kind of broken resemblance to the Son of God. . . .

For myself, I have uprightly labored to suit my endeavors to my pretences, and of later times (out of desire to attain their language) I have run through varieties of intercourses with them, day and night, summer and winter, by land and sea.

Many solemn discourses have I had with all sorts of nations of them, from one end of the country to another (so far as opportunity and the little language I have could reach).

I know there is no small preparation in the hearts of multitudes of them. I know their many solemn confessions to myself, and one to another, of their lost wandering conditions.

I know strong convictions upon the consciences of many of them, and their desires uttered that way.

I know not with how little knowledge and grace of Christ the Lord may save, and therefore neither will despair nor report much. . . . [2]

Now, because this is the great inquiry of all men, what Indians have been converted? what have the English done in those parts? what hopes of the Indians' receiving the knowledge of Christ? and because to this question, some put an edge from the boast of the Jesuits in Canada and Maryland, and especially from the wonderful conversions made by the Spaniards and Portugals in the West Indies, besides what I have here written, . . . I shall further present you with a brief additional discourse concerning this great point, being comfortably persuaded that that Father of spirits, who was graciously pleased to persuade Japhet (the gentiles) to dwell in the tents of Shem (the Jews), will in His holy season (I hope approaching) persuade these gentiles of America to partake of the mercies of Europe. And then shall be fulfilled what is written by the Prophet Malachi: "From the rising of the sun (in Europe) to the going down of the same (in America), my

name shall be great among the gentiles." So I desire to
hope and pray,

> Your unworthy countryman,
> *Roger Williams*

Taûbotne aunanamêan   *I thank you for your love.*

Observation

I have acknowledged amongst them an heart sensible of
kindnesses, and have reaped kindness again from many,
seven years after, when I myself had forgotten. Hence the
Lord Jesus exhorts his followers to do good for evil: for
otherwise sinners will do good for good, kindness for kindness.

Cowàmmaunsh	*I love you.*
Cowammaûnuck	*He loves you.*
Cowámmaus	*You are loving.*
Cowâutam?	*Understand you?*
Nowaûtam	*I understand.*
Cowâwtam tawhitche nippeeyaûmen?	*Do you know why I come?*
Cowannántam?	*Have you forgotten?*
Awanagusàntowosh	*Speak English*
Eeanàntowash	*Speak Indian.*
Cutehanshishaùmo?	*How many were you in company?*
Kúnnishishem?	*Are you alone?*
Nníshishem	*I am alone.*
Naneeshâumo	*There be two of us.*
Nanshwishâwmen	*We are four.*
Npiuckshâwmen	*We are ten.*
Neesneechecktashaûmen	*We are twenty.*
Nquitpausuckowashâwmen	*We are an hundred.*
Comishoonhómmis?	*Did you come by boat?*
Kuttiakewushaùmis?	*Came you by land?*

Mesh nomíshoonhómmin	*I came by boat.*
Meshntiauké wushem	*I came by land.*
Nippenowàntawem	*I am of another language.*
Penowantowawhettûock	*They are of a diverse language.*
Mat nowawtau hettémina	*We understand not each other.*
Nummaûchenèm	*I am sick.*
Cummaúchenem?	*Are you sick?*
Tashúckqunne cummauchenaûmis?	*How long have you been sick?*
Nummauchêmin, or Ntannetéimmin	*I will be going.*
Saûop Cummauchêmin	*You shall go tomorrow.*
Maúchish, or Ànakish	*Be going.*
Kuttannâwshesh	*Depart.*
Mauchéi, or Ànittui	*He is gone.*
Kautanaûshant	*He being gone.*
Mauchéhettit, or Kautanawshàwhettit	*When they are gone.*
Kukkowêtous	*I will lodge with you.*
Yò Cówish	*Do, lodge here.*
Howúnsheck	*Farewell.*
Chénock wonck cuppeeyeâumen?	*When will you be here again?*
Nétop tattà	*My friend, I cannot tell.*

From these courteous salutations, observe in general: there is a savor of civility and courtesy even amongst these wild Americans, both amongst themselves and towards strangers.

MORE PARTICULAR:

> The courteous pagan shall condemn
>   Uncourteous Englishmen,
> Who live like foxes, bears and wolves,
>   Or lion in his den.

Let none sing blessings to their souls,
  For that they courteous are:
The wild barbarians with no more
  Than nature go so far.

If nature's sons both wild and tame
  Humane and courteous be,
How ill becomes it sons of God
  To want humanity?

Parched meal, which is a ready wholesome food, which they eat with a little water, hot or cold. I have traveled with near 200 of them at once, near 100 miles through the woods, every man carrying a little basket of this at his back, and sometimes in a hollow leather girdle about his middle sufficient for a man three or four days.

With this ready provision, and their bow and arrows, are they ready for war and travel at an hour's warning. With a spoonful of this meal and a spoonful of water from the brook, have I made many a good dinner and supper.

Of eating and entertainment. If any stranger come in, they presently give him to eat of what they have; many a time, and at all times of the night (as I have fallen in travel upon their houses), when nothing hath been ready, they have themselves and their wives risen to prepare me some refreshing.

It is a strange truth that a man shall generally find more free entertainment and refreshing amongst these barbarians than amongst thousands that call themselves Christians.

MORE PARTICULAR:

Coarse bread and water's most their fare.
  O England's diet fine:

Thy cup runs o'er with plenteous store
  Of wholesome beer and wine.

Sometimes God gives them fish or flesh,
  Yet they're content without;
And what comes in, they part to friends
  And strangers round about.

God's providence is rich to His,
  Let none distrustful be;
In wilderness, in great distress,
  These ravens have fed me.

At whose house did you sleep? I once traveled to an island of the wildest in our parts, where in the night an Indian (as he said) had a vision or dream of the sun (whom they worship for a God) darting a beam into his breast, which he conceived to be the messenger of his death. This poor native called his friends and neighbors, and prepared some little refreshing for them, but himself was kept waking and fasting in great humiliations and invocations for ten days and nights. I was alone (having traveled from my bark, the wind being contrary), and little could I speak to them to their understandings, especially because of the change of their dialect or manner of speech from our neighbors; yet so much (through the help of God) I did speak, of the true and living only wise God, of the creation, of man, and his fall from God, &c., that at the parting many burst forth, "Oh when will you come again, to bring us more news of this God?"

From their sleeping. Sweet rest is not confined to soft beds, for not only God gives His beloved sleep on hard lodgings, but also nature and custom gives sound sleep to these Americans on the earth, on a board or mat. Yet how is Europe bound to God for better lodging?

MORE PARTICULAR:

> God gives them sleep on ground, on straw,
>   On sedgy mats or board:
> When English softest beds of down
>   Sometimes no sleep afford.

> I have known them leave their house and mat
>   To lodge a friend or stranger,
> When Jews and Christians oft have sent
>   Christ Jesus to the manger.

> 'Fore day they invocate their Gods,
>   Though many, false and new:
> O how should that God worshipped be
>   Who is but one and true?

The parts of the body. Nature knows no difference between Europe and Americans in blood, birth, bodies, God having of one blood made all mankind (Acts 17) and all by nature being children of wrath (Ephesians 2).

MORE PARTICULAR:

> Boast not, proud English, of thy birth and blood,
>   Thy brother Indian is by birth as good.
> Of one blood God made him and thee and all,
>   As wise, as fair, as strong, as personal.

> By nature, wrath's his portion, thine no more,
>   Till grace his soul and thine in Christ restore.
> Make sure thy second birth, else thou shalt see
>   Heaven ope to Indians wild, but shut to thee.

I am weary with speaking. Their manner is upon any tidings to sit round, double or treble or more, as their numbers be. I have seen near a thousand in a round, where English could not well near half so many have sitten. Every man hath his pipe of their tobacco, and deep silence they make, and attention give to him that speaketh; and many of them will deliver themselves, either in a relation of news or in a consultation, with very emphatical speech and great action, commonly an hour, and sometimes two hours together.

I hear you. They are impatient (as all men and God Himself is) when their speech is not attended and listened to.

I shall never believe it. As one answered me when I had discoursed about many points of God, of the creation, of the soul, of the danger of it and saving of it, he assented; but when I spake of the rising again of the body, he cried out, "I shall never believe this."

Of discourse and news. The whole race of mankind is generally infected with an itching desire of hearing news.

MORE PARTICULAR:

Man's restless soul hath restless eyes and ears,
Wanders in change of sorrows, cares and fears.
Fain would it (bee-like) suck by the ears, by the eye
Something that might his hunger satisfy:
The Gospel, or glad tiding only can
Make glad the English and the Indian.

A stone path. It is admirable to see what paths their naked hardened feet have made in the wilderness in most stony and rocky places.

Be my guide. The wilderness being so vast, it is a mercy that for a hire a man shall never want guides, who will carry provisions and such as hire them over the rivers and brooks, and find out often times hunting-houses or other lodgings at night.

Of travel. As the same sun shines on the wilderness that doth on a garden, so the same faithful and all-sufficient God can comfort-feed and safely guide even through a desolate, howling wilderness.

Of the weather. That judgment which the Lord Jesus pronounced against the weatherwise (but ignorant of the God of the weather) will fall most justly upon those natives and all men who are wise in natural things, but willingly blind in spiritual.

Of fowl. How sweetly do all the several sorts of heaven's birds, in all coasts of the world, preach unto men the praise of their maker's wisdom, power, and goodness, who feeds them and their young ones, summer and winter, with their several suitable sorts of food: although they neither sow nor reap, nor gather into barns!

Of the earth and the fruits thereof. God hath not left Himself without witness in all parts and coasts of the world: the rains and fruitful seasons, the earth, trees, plants, filling man's heart with food and gladness, witnesseth against, and condemneth man for his unthankfulness and unfruitfulness towards his maker.

Of beasts. The wilderness is a clear resemblance of the world, where greedy and furious men persecute and devour the harmless and innocent as the wild beasts pursue and devour the hinds and roes.

Of the sea. How unsearchable are the depths of the wisdom and power of God in separating from Europe,

Asia, and Africa such a mighty vast continent as America is? And that for so many ages? As also, by such a western ocean of about three thousand of English miles' breadth in passage over?

MORE PARTICULAR:

> They see God's wonders that are called
>   Through dreadful seas to pass,
> In tearing winds and roaring seas
>   And calms as smooth as glass.
>
> I have in Europe's ships oft been
>   In king of terrors' hand;
> When all have cried, "Now, now we sink,"
>   Yet God brought safe to land.
>
> Alone, 'mongst Indians in canoes,
>   Sometimes o'er-turned, I have been
> Half-inch from death, in ocean deep:
>   God's wonders I have seen.

Of fish and fishing. How may thousands of millions of those under water, sea-inhabitants, in all coasts of the world, preach to the sons of men on shore to adore their glorious maker by presenting themselves to Him as themselves (in a manner) present their lives from the wild ocean to the very doors of men, their fellow creatures in New England.

The Fire-God. When I have argued with them about their Fire-God: can it, say they, be but this fire must be a God or divine power, that out of a stone will arise in a spark, and when a poor naked Indian is ready to starve with cold in the house, and especially in the woods, often saves his life; doth dress all our food for us; and if it be

angry will burn the house about us; yea, if a spark fall into
the dry woods, burns up the country (though this burning
of the woods to them they count a benefit for destroying of
vermin, and keeping down the weeds and thickets)?

> Every little grass doth tell
> The sons of men, there God doth dwell.

Besides, there is a general custom amongst them, at the
apprehension of any excellency in men, women, birds,
beasts, fish, to cry out "Manittoo," that is, it is a God. As
thus if they see one man excell others in wisdom, valor,
strength, activity, they cry out, "Mannittoo," a God. And
therefore when they talk amongst themselves of the English ships, and great buildings, of the plowing of their
fields, and especially of books and letters, they will end
thus: "Manittowock," they are Gods; "Cummanitoo," you
are a God, &c. A strong conviction natural in the soul of
man, that God is filling all things, and places, and that all
excellencies dwell in God and proceed from Him, and that
they only are blessed who have that Jehovah their portion.

He is gone to the feast. They have a modest religious
persuasion not to disturb any man, either themselves, English, Dutch, or any, in their conscience and worship; and
therefore say, "Peace, hold your peace."

God's book or writing. After I had (as far as my language would reach) discoursed (upon a time) before the
chief sachem or prince of the country, with his archpriests
and many others in a full assembly; and being night,
wearied with travel and discourse, I lay down to rest; and
before I slept, I heard this passage:

A Qunnihticut Indian (who had heard our discourse)

told the sachem Miantonomu that souls went not up to heaven or down to hell: "For," saith he, "our fathers have told that our souls go to the southwest."

The sachem answered, "But how do you know yourself that your souls go to the southwest; did you ever see a soul go thither?"

The native replied, "When did he (meaning myself) see a soul go to heaven or hell?"

The sachem again replied, "He hath books and writings, and one which God Himself made, concerning men's souls, and therefore may well know more than we that have none, but take all upon trust from our forefathers."

The said sachem and the chief of his people discoursed by themselves of keeping the Englishman's day of worship, which I could easily have brought the country to but that I was persuaded, and am, that God's way is first to turn a soul from its idols, both of heart, worship, and conversation, before it is capable of worship to the true and living God. . . . As also that the two first principles and foundations of true religion or worship of the true God in Christ are repentance from dead works, and faith towards God, before the doctrine of baptism or washing and laying on of hands, which contain the ordinances and practices of worship: the want of which, I conceive, is the bane of millions of souls in England and all other nations professing to be Christian nations, who are brought by public authority to baptism and fellowship with God in ordinances of worship before the saving work of repentance and a true turning to God.

The whole world shall ere long be burned. Upon the relating that God hath once destroyed the world by water, and that He will visit it the second time with consuming fire, I have been asked this profitable question of some of them: "What then will become of us? Where then shall we be?"

Of their government and justice. I could never discern that excess of scandalous sins amongst them which Europe aboundeth with. Drunkenness and gluttony, generally they know not what sins they be; and although they have not so much to restrain them (both in respect of knowledge of God and laws of men) as the English have, yet a man shall never hear of such crimes amongst them, of robberies, murders, adulteries, &c., as amongst the English. I conceive that the glorious sun of so much truth as shines in England hardens our English hearts; for what the sun softeneth not, it hardens.

Of their trading. O, the infinite wisdom of the most holy, wise God, who hath so advanced Europe above America that there is not a sorry hoe, hatchet, knife, nor a rag of cloth in all America but what comes over the dreadful Atlantic Ocean from Europe! And yet, that Europe be not proud nor America discouraged: what treasures are hid in some parts of America and in our New English parts? How have foul hands (in smoky houses) the first handling of those furs which are after worn upon the hands of queens and heads of princes?

I will owe it you. They are very desirous to come into debt, but then he that trusts them must sustain a twofold loss:

First, of his commodity;

Secondly, of his custom, as I have found by dear experience. Some are ingenuous, plain-hearted, and honest; but the most never pay unless a man follow them to their several abodes, towns, and houses, as I myself have been forced to do, which hardship and travels it hath yet pleased God to sweeten with some experiences and some little gain of language.

I have found a deer, which sometimes they do, taking a wolf in the very act of his greedy prey, when sometimes (the wolf being greedy of his prey) they kill him. Sometimes the wolf, having glutted himself with the one half, leaves the other for his next bait; but the glad Indian, finding of it, prevents him.

And that we may see how true it is that all wild creatures, and many tame, prey upon the poor deer (which are there in a right emblem of God's persecuted, that is, hunted people:

> To harmless roes and does,
> Both wild and tame are foes).

I remember how a poor deer was long hunted and chased by a wolf; at last (as their manner is) after the chase of ten, it may be more, miles' running, the stout wolf tired out the nimble deer, and seizing upon it, killed: in the act of devouring his prey, two English swine, big with pig, passed by, assaulted the wolf, drove him from his prey, and devoured so much of that poor deer as they both surfeited and died that night.

The wolf is an emblem of a fierce, blood-sucking persecutor.

The swine of a covetous, rooting worldling. Both make a prey of the Lord Jesus and His poor servants.

Of their hunting. There is a blessing upon endeavor, even to the wildest Indians; the sluggard roasts not that which he took in hunting, but the substance of the diligent (either in earthly or heavenly affairs) is precious.

Of their gaming. This life is a short minute, eternity follows. On the improvement or dis-improvement of this short minute depends a joyful or dreadful eternity. Yet (which I tremble to think of) how cheap is this invaluable jewel, and how many vain inventions and foolish pastimes have the sons of men in all parts of the world found out, to pass time and post over this short minute of life, until like some pleasant river they have past into *mare mortuum,* the dead sea of eternal lamentation.

Of their war. How dreadful and yet how righteous is it with the most righteous judge of the whole world, that all the generations of men being turned enemies against, and fighting against Him who gives them breath and being and all things (whom yet they cannot reach), should stab, kill, burn, murder, and devour each other?

Of death and burial. O, how terrible is the look, the speedy and serious thought of death to all the sons of men? Thrice happy those who are dead and risen with the Son of God, for they are passed from death to life and shall not see death (a heavenly sweet paradox or riddle), as the Son of God hath promised them.

MORE PARTICULAR:

> The Indians say their bodies die,
>   Their souls they do not die;
> Worse are than Indians such as hold
>   The soul's mortality.
>
> Our hopeless body rots, say they,
>   Is gone eternally.
> English hope better, yet some's hope
>   Proves endless misery.

Two worlds of men shall rise and stand
  'Fore Christ's most dreadful bar:
Indians and English naked too,
  That now most gallant are.

True Christ most glorious then shall make
  New earth, and heavens new;
False Christs, false Christians then shall quake.
  O blessed then the true!

Now, to the most high and most holy, immortal, invisible and only wise God, who alone is Alpha and Omega, the beginning and the ending, the first and last, who was and is and is to come; from whom, and by whom, and to whom are all things; by whose gracious assistance and wonderful supportment in so many varieites of hardship and outward miseries I have had such converse with barbarous nations, and have been mercifully assisted to frame this poor *Key,* which may (through His blessing, in His own holy season) open a door, yea, doors of unknown mercies to us and them, be honor, glory, power, riches, wisdom, goodness, and dominion ascribed by all His in Jesus Christ to eternity. *Amen.*

IV Prophet in Metropolis

I

IN THE SUMMER of 1636, in his refuge at Providence—having survived the terrible winter with the help of only God and a few stray Indians—Roger Williams had in his hands three documents that humiliated and outraged him.

First, he had a manuscript which John Cotton had written during the winter (either when Williams was in the thick of his fight at Salem or else when he was shivering in the wilderness), the "Answer" to four chapters in a book presented to him for comment by one John Hall, of Roxbury. *A Most Humble Supplication of the King's Majesty's Loyal Subjects* was printed (no doubt surreptitiously) in 1620, purporting to be written by an Anabaptist imprisoned, as he said, "for his conscience," in Newgate. Deprived of ink, he penned his thoughts with milk and smuggled out the pages to his fellows. Cotton, newly installed in the foremost position in the colony—teacher of the Church of Boston—pontifically replied in accents revealing that he already assumed himself to be dean of the colonial clergy; his reply did not quite satisfy Hall (who later moved to Connecticut), and so Hall sent the manuscript to Williams, who had time to ponder it.

The second document was a treatise of eleven "heads," each buttressed with copious quotation from Scripture, sent by the associated ministers of Massachusetts Bay to the people of Salem in the autumn of 1635. Williams had not seen it in Salem, but he knew it had been effective in persuading a majority of the congregation to turn against him. Entitled *A Model of Church and Civil Power*, it was a concise summary of the position Massachusetts had arrived at in the philosophy of church and state, after having by the act of migration completed its revolution and stabilized itself on the basis of a Nonseparatist orthodoxy. Cotton, we know, had nothing to do with writing it, but Williams believed that he did. Williams wanted to see it, and in the summer Elder Sharpe sent him a copy from Salem.

The third document was by far the most galling: it was a haughty letter written directly to Williams by John Cotton himself, in this same summer, telling him why he was banished, exulting in the sentence, and calling on him to repent. It was a calculated insult, striking a man who was down and all but out.

What the three added up to showed, or seemed to show, that not only was John Cotton the most implacable of Williams' foes but that he was the mainspring of a malignant conspiracy in Boston which would not rest until they had destroyed him. There were many reasons why between these two the struggle should be unto the death. In the first place, back in Essex before the migration Williams had dared rebuke the great and much-esteemed Cotton for complying with the Book of Common Prayer. Secondly, Cotton now occupied the throne in Boston which could have been Williams' had Williams not refused it out of a scruple of conscience; where Cotton now lorded it, Williams could have strutted had he been able to swallow the casuistry of Nonseparation.

Furthermore, there is the still deeper reason: Cotton had shown himself in theology the least legalistic, the most responsive to allegories and typologies, of all theologians who came to New England.[1] Williams would know better than to suppose that down-to-earth federalists like Thomas Hooker would have anything but contempt for his inspired readings of the Bible, but something more might be expected of Cotton, on whom Hooker had long looked askance. Like Mrs. Hutchinson, Williams expected Cotton to live up to the vision he imparted to his followers. Cotton failed Williams, as the next year he also failed Anne Hutchinson; henceforth the very existence of these two was for him a standing rebuke. Williams' grief over what he considered this betrayal was profound, but Cotton's hatred became a family heirloom, to be passed on to his sons and grandsons (see pages 235-240).

But still the deepest of all reasons for this hostility was the fact that Cotton, so widely renowned among Puritans in England and Calvinists on the Continent, became the symbol of the New England Way. More than any other he assured the world that a Congregational system could get along with, indeed required, a vigorous magistracy, that churches founded on an exclusive covenant and consisting only of tried saints were entirely compatible with a forcible and intolerant rule of uniformity. He was the incarnation of that image of respectability, conformity, success (all the more because he was supposed in his youth to have been radical and to have suffered for nonconformity), which has since dominated American spiritual and intellectual life. Williams is the first in our history to rebel against this exemplar, to prefer going into the wilderness out of devotion to an idea which men like Cotton could grandly explain was altogether crack-brained and not to be taken seriously.

For seven years Williams was too much occupied with earning a bare living, and then with trying to control the mob which year after year descended on his colony, to find time for replying to the three documents. Besides, there would be no way of publishing anything in the wilderness, and not enough of an audience for him to have any effect on his day and age. However, in order to prepare in his mind what he might say if he ever got the chance, he needed no library beyond his Bible and no study beyond his canoe or his nights of meditation by Indian fires. There is something both sublime and pathetic in his cherishing these documents long after the authors had forgotten them, hoarding his thoughts until God's providence gave him his opportunity. He must have mulled them over until he knew every paragraph by heart.

The final publication of his retorts gives evidence of hasty writing and of still more hasty printing, but the words had been so long formulated and treasured up that Williams could indeed throw them pell-mell upon the paper. He was not a man of many ideas, and the intense concentration of these years centered him even more narrowly on the three or four he did possess. They are all present, at least by implication, in the *Key*, and they are asserted over and over again in the following works. Williams had the sort of mind which, once convinced, finds that truth improves with repetition.

On arriving in London, he evidently gave his first

thought to printing the *Key*, which appeared on September
7, 1643. He could hardly have made a cleverer tactical
move, for the book made him overnight a voice in the
metropolis. At this moment the Puritans, fighting a war
that was not going well, had appealed to the Scots, who
were demanding a large price for their assistance. On
July 1 Parliament had summoned the Westminster Assembly, to consist of leading divines of both kingdoms, commis-
sioned to prepare a model of orthodox polity and doctrine—to do on a large scale what the Massachusetts clergy
had done in preparing for Salem's benefit the *Model* Williams was still preserving. On September 25 Parliament
signed the Solemn League and Covenant, which definitely
committed it to impose by force on all England (or on as
much as Parliamentary troops could wrest from the Cav-
aliers) an ecclesiastical regime similar to that of Scotland.

But at this point, to almost everybody's surprise and to
the consternation of Presbyterians and Scots, five theologians in the Assembly who, because of their fame and their
scholarship, could not be excluded, arose to dissent; in
their *Apologeticall Narration* they declared that the true
form of Biblical polity was not Presbyterian but Congregational—exactly that of New England, exactly that of the
manuscript *Model* in Williams' baggage—and they were
prepared to fight against the majority of their brothers
more resolutely and furiously than against King Charles
himself.

These five had spent their exile in Holland; they had
several times been on the point of giving up Europe for
lost and joining their friends—the chief of whom was Cotton—in America. Now, with Puritans falling every day into
the Independent ranks—earnest students of the Bible who

hitherto had not critically studied the New Testament and had assumed that it taught Presbyterianism, but who in the freedom of the wars were listening to the arguments and becoming persuaded that God's intention was Congregational—with this increasing support, the five brethren had become a power in the land out of all proportion to their numbers. At this point (the five were soon to undergo surprising developments) their Independency had no place for liberty of conscience. On the contrary, they paid profuse tribute to the success of New England in maintaining orthodoxy and suppressing such heretics as Williams; they explicitly promised that once they got power they no less than the Presbyterians would reduce all England to a unified discipline. They denied that they were or ever had been Separatists. They promised, in short, to make England another Massachusetts.

A terrifying prospect of another of the Reformation's battles between absolutes, between Presbyterians and Independents, now opened, promising to split the nation even more disastrously than did the conflict between King and Parliament. Roger Williams, working on his long-accumulated replies to New England, felt that he, and as always he alone, could tell the Independents what they were rushing toward. While writing with one hand against Cotton, with the other, so to speak, he composed *Queries of Highest Consideration,* addressed it to the five Independents, and got it through the press by February 9, 1644.

Circumstances and the narrowness of his range make the entire writings of Roger Williams a single, sustained oratorio, of which the *Key* may be viewed as a sort of overture. The *Queries* proclaim at once his major themes. To the majority in Parliament, to all Presbyterians, and as yet

to most Independents, the book would seem a weird pro-
duction, asserting in the disarming form of questions that
not only should Presbyterians and Independents refrain
from cutting each other's throats, but that even Catholics
should be tolerated. It suggested that the very effort to
set up the pure church—even assuming one knew what
a pure church ought to be—was unchristian, that it was in
effect to reconstitute the Court of High Commission which
Parliament had exultantly abolished in July 1641. To all
but a few in London in February 1644, this prophet who
had lived with Indians spoke a language as barbaric as that
which he had transcribed in the *Key*, especially at the end
of the *Queries* when he reinforced his absurd ideas by the
still more absurd notion that Israel was a "type" and therefore not to be imitated by Parliament or by the Assembly—
or by the New Model Army.

Queries of Highest Consideration, Proposed to

Mr. Tho. Goodwin   *Mr. Jer. Burroughs*
Mr. Phillip Nye   *Mr. Sidr. Simpson*
Mr. Wil. Bridges

And

To the Commissioners from the General Assembly
(so called) of the Church of Scotland
London, 1644

To the Right Honorable both Houses of the High Court
of Parliament.

Right Honorable:

IT IS a woeful privilege attending all great states and personages that they seldom hear any other music but what is known will please them.

Though our music sound not sweet but harsh, yet please you to know it is not fitted to your ears but to your hearts, and the bleeding heart of this afflicted nation. . . .

Most renowned patriots, you sit at helm in as great a storm as e'er poor England's commonwealth was lost in. . . . You will please to say: "We are constantly told, and we believe it, that religion is our first care, and reformation of that our greatest task."

Right Honorable, your wisdoms know the fatal miscarriages of England's Parliaments in this point; what setting up, pulling down, what formings, reformings, and again deformings, to admiration. . . .

It shall never be your honor to this or future ages to be confined to the patterns of either French, Dutch, Scotch, or New-English churches. We humbly conceive some higher act concerning religion attends and becomes your consultations. If He whose name is Wonderful Counselor be consulted and obeyed according to His last will and testament (as you may please in the queries to view), we are confident you shall exceed the acts and patterns of all neighbor nations, highly exalt the name of the Son of God, provide for the peace of this distracted state, engage the souls of all that fear God to give thanks and supplicate for you, further the salvation of thousands, and leave the sweet perfume of your names precious to all succeeding generations. . . .

Query II. Whereas you both agree (though with some difference) that the civil magistrate must reform the church, establish religion, and so consequently must first judge and judicially determine which is true, which is false: or else must implicitly believe as the Assembly believes and take it upon trust; and so consequently is he the head, root, and fountain of the supremacy of all spiritual power and hath the power of keys, of opening and shutting heaven's gates? (Of which power, upon a grudge (as 'tis said) about his wife, King Henry despoiled the pope, and with the consent and act of Parliament, sat down himself in the pope's chair in England, as since his successors have done.)

We now query, since the Parliament (being the representative commonwealth) hath no other power but what the commonweal derive unto and betrust it with, whether it will not evidently follow that the commonweal, the nation, the kingdom, and (if it were in Augustus his time) the whole world, must rule and govern the church, and Christ Himself, as the church is called?

Furthermore, if the Honorable Houses (the representative commonweal) shall erect a spiritual court for the judging of spiritual men and spiritual causes (although a new name be put upon it, yet), whether or no such a court is not in the true nature and kind of it an High Commission? And is not this a reviving of Moses and the sanctifying of a new land of Canaan, of which we hear nothing in the testament of Christ Jesus, nor of any other holy nation, but the particular church of Christ?

Is not this to subject this holy nation, this heavenly Jerusalem, the wife and spouse of Jesus, the pillar and ground of truth, to the vain, uncertain, and changeable mutations of this present evil world?

Who knows not in how few years the commonweal of

England hath set up and pulled down? The fathers made the children heretics, and the children the fathers. How doth the Parliament in Henry VIII his days condemn the absolute Popery in Henry VII? How is in Edward VI his time the Parliament of Henry VIII condemned for their half-Popery, half-Protestantism? How soon doth Queen Mary's Parliament condemn Edward for his absolute Protestantism? And Elizabeth's Parliament as soon condemn Queen Mary's for their absolute Popery? 'Tis true, Queen Elizabeth made laws against Popery and Papists, but the government of bishops, the Common Prayer, the ceremonies, were then so high in that Queen's and Parliament's eye that the members of this present and ever-renowned Parliament would have then been counted little less than heretics.[2] And oh! since the commonweal cannot without a spiritual rape force the consciences of all to one worship, oh, that it may never commit that rape in forcing the consciences of all men to one worship which a stronger arm and sword may soon (as formerly) arise to alter.

Query IV. Whether in your consciences before God you be not persuaded (notwithstanding your promiscuous joining with all) that few of the people of England and Scotland, and fewer of the nobles and gentry, are such spiritual matter, living stones, truly regenerate and converted; and therefore, whether it be not the greatest courtesy in the world which you may possibly perform unto them to acquaint them impartially with their conditions and how impossible it is for a dead stone to have fellowship with the living God, and for any man to enter into the Kingdom of God without a second birth? . . .

Query VIII. Whether, although (as is expressed) the
godly in the three kingdoms desire a reformation, yet since
the Lamb of God and Prince of peace hath not in His testament given us a pattern, precept, or promise for the under-
taking of a civil war for his sake: we query how with comfort to your souls you may encourage the English treasure
to be exhausted, and the English blood to be spilt for the
cause of Christ? We readily grant the civil magistrate
armed by God with a civil sword to execute vengeance
against robbers, murderers, tyrants. Yet where it merely
concerns Christ, we find when His Disciples desire vengeance upon offenders, He meekly answers, "You know not
what spirit you are of; I came not to destroy men's lives,
but to save them." . . .

We query (if security may be taken by the wisdom of
the state for civil subjection) why even the Papists themselves and their consciences may not be permitted in the
world? For otherwise, if England's government were the
government of the whole world, not only they, but a world
of idolaters of all sorts, yea the whole world, must be
driven out of the world?

We query whether the common body of Protestants,
impenitent and unregenerate, be not further off salvation,
and lie not under a greater guilt, than does the body of
ignorant Papists? And we humbly desire it may be deeply
pondered what should be the kindling of the jealousy of
God, to pour forth the blood of so many thousand of Protestants by the bloody hands of the Papists (since most just
He is, and righteous in all His judgments): whether or no
the laws enacted and violence offered even to the consciences of the Papists themselves have not kindled these
devouring flames? . . .

Query XII. Since you profess to want more light, and that a greater light is yet to be expected—yea, that the Church of Scotland may yet have need of a greater reformation—we query how you can profess and swear to persecute all others as schismatics, heretics, &c., that believe they see a further light and dare not join with either of your churches? Whether the Lamb's wife have received any such commission or disposition from the Lamb her husband so to practice? . . . It being the nature only of a wolf to hunt the lambs and sheep, but impossible for a lamb or sheep, or a thousand flocks of sheep, to persecute one wolf? (We speak of spiritual sheep and spiritual wolves, for other wolves against the civil state, we profess it to be the duty of the civil state to persecute and suppress them.) . . .

Whether there can possibly be expected the least look of peace in these fatal distractions and tempests raised but by taking counsel of the great and wisest politician that ever was, the Lord Jesus Christ, in this particular?

We know the allegations against this counsel: the head of all is that from Moses (not Christ) his pattern in the typical land of Canaan, the kings of Israel and Judah. We humbly desire it may be searched into, and we believe it will be found but one of Moses' shadows, vanished at the coming of the Lord Jesus: yet such a shadow as is directly opposite to the very testament and coming of the Lord Jesus. Opposite to the very nature of a Christian church, the only holy nation and Israel of God. Opposite to the very tender bowels of humanity (how much more of Christianity?), abhorring to pour out the blood of men merely for their souls' belief and worship. Opposite to the very essentials and fundamentals of the nature of a civil magistracy, a civil commonweal or combination of men, which can only respect civil things. Opposite to the Jews' conversion to Christ, by not permitting them a civil life or being. Opposite to the civil peace, and the lives of millions slaughtered upon this ground, in mutual persecuting each other's conscience, especially the Protestant and the Papist. Opposite to the souls of all men who by persecution are ravished into a dissembled worship which their hearts embrace not. Opposite to the best of God's servants, who in all Popish and Protestant states have been commonly esteemed and persecuted as the only schismatics, heretics, &c. Opposite to that light of Scripture which is expected yet to shine, which must by that doctrine be suppressed as a new or old heresy or novelty. All this in all ages experience testifies, which never saw any long-lived fruit of peace or righteousness to grow upon that fatal tree.

II

Meanwhile, amid many distractions, Williams was perfecting his triple assault on Cotton. Obviously he would want to start with the wounding letter Cotton had inflicted on him, but the difficulty was, of course, that nobody knew about the letter. Williams would have cut a foolish figure had he opened his attack on an epistle seven years forgotten. But then, as though by a special "overruling" act of Providence, shortly after the *Key* had attracted attention to Williams, there mysteriously appeared on the London bookstalls *A Letter of Mr. John Cottons, Teacher of the Church in Boston, in New-England, to Mr. Williams a Preacher there.* Cotton's name was such that all the world—or at least the Puritan world—read and then waited. Williams could now command an audience, and applied himself with satisfaction, we might almost say with glee, to preparing his long-meditated reply. In fact, he himself tells us with just what eagerness he worked:

I rejoice in the goodness and wisdom of Him who is the Father of light and mercies, in ordering the season both of mine own present opportunity of answer, as also, and especially of such protestations and resolutions of so many fearing God, to seek what worship and worshippers are acceptable to Him in Jesus Christ.

On February 5, 1644 (four days before the *Queries*, so that the two made a virtually simultaneous impression), *Mr. Cottons Letter Lately Printed, Examined and Answered* was published.

Williams usually exhibits the gentleness of the dove, but on occasion the cunning of the serpent. He blandly asserts that he was not responsible for letting Cotton's *Letter* get out—"by whose procurement I know not." He was bound to know that, as Cotton later understated it, when copies reached Boston, Cotton would find them "unwelcome news." Cotton insinuated that Williams must have known what was happening, but pretended to believe Williams' story in order the more vehemently to deride him for taking advantage of this trick: "So a bird of prey, affecting to soar aloft, getteth first upon the top of a molehill, and from thence taketh his rise from pale to tree, till he have surmounted the highest mountains." But that Cotton was obliged to respond shows how effective was Williams' timing: Cotton's *Letter* of 1636 could hardly be broadcast at a more embarrassing moment for Massachusetts.

Despite admiring tributes in the *Apologeticall Narration* to the orthodoxy of New England, it was already becoming apparent to many Independents (particularly to General

Oliver Cromwell) that if they were to survive against the Presbyterian majority, they would have to construct a working alliance with the now numerous and vigorous sects. Every one of these gloried in the name of Separatist, and for the Independents to close with them would mean to loosen, if not more, their ties with New England. To bring Cotton's rigorous Nonseparatism, along with its consequent intolerance, to light in the London of 1643 was at one and the same time to strike a blow against the more dogmatic Independents and against orthodox New England. It was also to gain the greatest possible publicity for Roger Williams.

Cotton's *Letter* confirms our suspicions that he was caught in a vise of conscience concerning Williams. He says he took no part in banishing Williams, but goes out of his way to say that he approved. In case Williams does not realize why the expulsion, Cotton will tell him that it was not because of his annoying foibles, but simply and solely for his Separatism. Clearly Cotton is goaded to writing this unnecessary letter because he must apologize for himself: public announcement of separation from the Church of England is not required of New Englanders because the "substance of true repentance" is adequate. It is not necessary that saints be "convinced of the sinfulness of every sipping of the whore's cup"—in fact, they can be church members even though they have more than sipped. Only "overheated" fanatics demand an unrealistic sanctity. New England is highly sane: it walks between the two extremes of the parish system and doctrinaire separation. Separatists are arrogant, self-opinionated; they and Williams will better serve the great cause if they give over their conceit and pitch in "to help the Lord against the mighty, to wit, either against the high prelates or against the inventions of men."

But thousands in the altered climate of London in 1643 could see, as clearly as we do today, that Cotton, even though he had escaped to the security of Boston, had written that *Letter* out of insecurity. All the more reason why they waited with curiosity, and even amusement, for Williams' examination. He did not disappoint them.

Most of Williams' examination is an attack on the logic, or lack of logic, in the Nonseparatist position, and so makes dull reading today. What is worth salvaging from this ecclesiastical pedantry is the conception Williams extracted out of Congregational theory of the truly independent church. By a process which we may venture to call extrapolation, he projected the covenant, the principles of consent and of Congregational autonomy into the vision of such a church as (perhaps) never yet existed and which might never physically exist, but which, in its utter refusal to compromise, to yield to politics or to expedience, becomes the only reliable measure of the Christian community. And in the last pages, Williams again—although still not pressing the point too hard—intimates that he who falls short of the typological interpretation of Israel is foredoomed to fall short of the true standard of Christianity.

Mr. Cottons Letter Lately Printed,
Examined and Answered
By Roger Williams of Providence in New-England
London, 1644

To the impartial reader:
THIS LETTER I acknowledge to have received from Mr. Cotton (whom for his personal excellencies I truly honor

and love). Yet at such a time of distressed wandering amongst the barbarians that, being destitute of food, of clothes, of time, I reserved it (though hardly, amidst so many barbarous distractions), and afterward prepared an answer to be returned.

In the interim, some friends being much grieved that one publicly acknowledged to be godly and dearly beloved should yet be so exposed to the mercy of an howling wilderness, in frost and snow, Mr. Cotton, to take off the edge of censure from himself, professed both in speech and writing that he was no procurer of my sorrows.

Some letters then passed between us, in which I proved and expressed that if I had perished in that sorrowful winter's flight, only the blood of Jesus Christ could have washed him from the guilt of mine.

His final answer was, "Had you perished, your blood had been on your own head; it was your sin to procure it, and your sorrow to suffer it."[3]

Here I confess I stopped, and ever since suppressed mine answer, waiting if it might please the Father of mercies more to mollify and soften, and render more humane and merciful, the ear and heart of that (otherwise) excellent and worthy man. . . .

Mr Cotton, beloved in Christ:

THOUGH I humbly desire to acknowledge myself unworthy to be beloved, and most of all unworthy of the name of Christ and to be beloved for His sake, yet since Mr. Cotton is pleased to use such an affectionate compellation and testimonial expression to one so afflicted and persecuted by himself and others (whom for their personal worth and godliness I also honor and love), I desire it may be seriously reviewed by himself and them, and all men, whether the Lord Jesus be well pleased that one, beloved in Him, should (for no other cause than shall presently appear) be denied the common air to breath in and a civil cohabitation upon the same common earth? Yea, and also without mercy and humane compassion be exposed to winter miseries in a howling wilderness? . . .

I observe his charge against me for not harkening to a twofold voice of Christ: first, of the whole church of Christ with me.

Unto which I answer according to my conscience and persuasion. I was then charged by office with the feeding of that flock, and when in the apprehension of some public evils the whole country professed to humble itself and seek God, I endeavored (as a faithful watchman on the walls) to sound the trumpet and give the alarm; and upon a fast day, in faithfulness and uprightness (as then and still I am persuaded), I discovered eleven public sins for which I believed (and do) it pleased God to inflict and further to threaten public calamities: most of which eleven (if not all) that church then seemed to assent unto, until afterward in my troubles the greater part of that church was swayed and bowed (whether for fear of persecution or otherwise) to say and practice what, to my knowledge, with sighs and groans many of them mourned under. . . .

For my not harkening to the second voice—the testimony of so many elders and brethren of other churches: because I truly esteem and honor the persons of which the New English churches are constituted, I will not answer the argument of number and multitudes against one, as we use to answer the Popish universality, that God sometimes stirs up one Elijah against 800 of Baal's priests, one Micaiah against 400 of Ahab's prophets, one Athanasius against many hundreds of Arian bishops, one John Huss against the whole Council of Constance, Luther and the two witnesses against many thousands. Yet this I may truly say, that David himself and the princes of Israel and thirty thousand Israel, carrying up the Ark, were not to be harkened to nor followed in their (as I may say) holy rejoicings and triumphings: the due order of the Lord yet being wanting to their holy intentions and affections, and the Lord at last sending in a sad stop and breach of Uzzah amongst them *(Perez Uzzah),* as He hath ever yet done and will do in all the reformations that have been hitherto made by His Davids which are not after the due order.[4] To which purpose it is maintained by the Papists themselves and by their councils that Scripture only must be heard—yea, one Scripture in the mouth of one simple mechanic before the whole council. By that only do I desire to stand or fall in trial or judgment: for all flesh is grass, and the beauty of flesh (the most wisest, holiest, learnedest) is but the flower or beauty of grass, only the word of Jehovah standeth fast for ever. . . .

Mr. Cotton endeavoreth to discover the sandiness of those grounds out of which (as he saith) I have banished myself.

I answer, I question not his holy and loving intentions and affections, and that my grounds seem sandy to himself and others. Those intentions and affections may be accepted (as his person) with the Lord, as David of his desires to build the Lord a temple, though on sandy grounds. Yet Mr. Cotton's endeavors to prove the firm rock of the truth of Jesus to be the weak and uncertain sand of man's invention—those shall perish and burn like hay or stubble. The rocky strength of those grounds shall more appear in the Lord's season, and himself may yet confess so much, as since he came into New England he hath confessed the sandiness of the grounds of many of his practices in which he walked in old England, and the rockiness of their grounds that witnessed against them and himself in those practices, though for that time their grounds seemed sandy to him. . . .

After my public trial and answers at the General Court, one of the most eminent magistrates[5] (whose name and speech may by others be remembered) stood up and spake:

"Mr. Williams," saith he, "holds forth these four particulars:

"First, that we have not our land by patent from the King but that the natives are the true owners of it, and that we ought to repent of such a receiving it by patent.

"Secondly, that it is not lawful to call a wicked person to swear, to pray, as being actions of God's worship.

"Thirdly, that it is not lawful to hear any of the ministers of the parish assemblies in England.

"Fourthly, that the civil magistrate's power extends only to the bodies and goods and outward state of men."

I acknowledge the particulars were rightly summed up, and I also hope that as I then maintained the rocky strength of them to my own and other consciences' satisfaction, so (through the Lord's assistance) I shall be ready for the same grounds not only to be bound and banished but to die also in New England as for most holy truths of God in Christ Jesus.

"Yea but," saith he, "upon those grounds you banished yourself from the society of the churches in these countries."

I answer, if Mr. Cotton mean my own voluntary with-
drawing from those churches resolved to continue in those
evils and persecuting the witnesses of the Lord presenting
light unto them, I confess it was my own voluntary act.
Yea, I hope the act of the Lord Jesus sounding forth in me,
a poor despised ram's horn, the blast which shall in His
own holy season cast down the strength and confidence of
those inventions of men in the worshipping of the true and
living God. And lastly, His act in enabling me to be faithful in any measure to suffer such great and mighty trials
for His name's sake.

But if by banishing myself he intend the act of civil
banishment from their common earth and air, I then observe with grief the language of the dragon in a lamb's lip.
Among other expressions of the dragon, are not these common to the witnesses of the Lord Jesus rent and torn by
his persecutions: "Go now, say you are persecuted, you are
persecuted for Christ, suffer for your conscience: No, it is
your schism, heresy, obstinacy; the Devil hath deceived
thee, thou hast justly brought this upon thee, thou has
banished thyself, &c." Instances are abundant in so many
books of martyrs and the experience of all men, and therefore I spare to recite in so short a treatise.

Secondly, if he mean this civil act of banishing, why
should he call a civil sentence from the civil state, within
a few weeks' execution in so sharp a time of New England's
cold, why should he call this a banishment from the
churches except he silently confess that the frame or constitution of their churches is implicitly national (which yet
they profess against)? For otherwise, why was I not yet
permitted to live in the world or commonweal except for
this reason, that the commonweal and church is yet but

one, and he that is banished from the one must necessarily be banished from the other also? . . .

For myself, I acknowledge it a blessed gift of God to be enabled to suffer and to be banished for His name's sake. And yet I doubt not to affirm that Mr. Cotton himself would have counted it a mercy if he might have practiced in old England what now he doth in New, with the enjoyment of the civil peace, safety, and protection of the state.

Or, should he dissent from the New English churches and join in worship with some other (as some few years since he was upon the point to do in a separation from the churches there as legal[6]), would he count it a mercy to be plucked up by the roots, him and his, to endure the losses, distractions, miseries that do attend such a condition? The truth is, both the mother and the daughter, old and New England, for the countries and governments, are lands and governments incomparable: and might it please God to persuade the mother to permit the inhabitants of New England, her daughter, to enjoy their conscience to God after a particular Congregational way, and to persuade the daughter to permit the inhabitants of the mother, old England, to walk there after their conscience in a parishional way (which yet neither mother nor daughter is persuaded to permit), I conceive Mr. Cotton himself, were he seated in old England again, would not count it a mercy to be banished from the civil state.

And therefore (lastly), as he casts dishonor upon the name of God to make Him the author of such cruel mercy, so had his soul been in my soul's case—exposed to the miseries, poverties, necessities, wants, debts, hardships of sea and land, in a banished condition—he would, I pre-

sume, reach forth a more merciful cordial to the afflicted.
But he that is despised and afflicted is like a lamp despised
in the eyes of him that is at ease. . . .

Mr. Cotton proceedeth: "The second stumbling block or
offense which you have taken at the way of these churches
is that you conceive us to walk between Christ and Antichrist . . . in practicing separation here, and not repenting
of our preaching and printing against it in our own country."

Unto this he answers that they halt not but walk in the
midst of two extremes, the one of being defiled with the
pollution of other churches, the other of renouncing the
churches for the remnants of pollutions.

This moderation he (with ingenuous moderation) professeth he sees no cause to repent of.

Answer: With the Lord's gracious assistance, we shall
prove this middle walking to be no less than halting, for
which we shall show cause of repentance, beseeching Him
that is a Prince and a Savior to give repentance unto his
Israel.

First, Mr. Cotton himself confesseth that no national,
provincial, diocesan, or parish church (wherein some truly
godly are not) are true churches. Secondly, he practiceth
no church estate but such as is constituted only of godly
persons nor admitteth any unregenerate or ungodly person. Thirdly, he confesseth a church of Christ cannot be
constituted of such godly persons who are in bondage to
the inordinate love of the world. Fourthly, if a church consist of such, God's people ought to separate from them.

Upon these his own confessions, I earnestly beseech Mr.
Cotton and all that fear God to ponder how he can say he
walks with an even foot between two extremes when, ac-

cording to his own confession, national churches, parish churches, yea a church constituted of godly persons given to inordinate love of the world, are false and to be separated from? And yet he will not have the parish church to be separated from for the remnant of pollution (I conceive he meaneth ceremonies and bishops), notwithstanding that he also acknowledgeth that the generality of every parish in England consisteth of unregenerate persons and of thousands inbondaged not only to worldliness but also ignorance, superstition, scoffing, swearing, cursing, whoredom, drunkenness, theft, lying. What are two or three, or more, of regenerate and godly persons in such communions but as two or three roses or lilies in a wilderness, a few grains of good corn in a heap of chaff, a few sheep among herds of wolves or swine or (if more civil) flocks of goats, a little good dough swallowed up with a whole bushel of leaven, or a little precious gold confounded and mingled with a whole heap of dross? The searcher of all hearts knows I write not this to reproach any, knowing that myself am by nature a child of wrath and that the Father of mercies shows mercy to whom and when He will: but for the name of Christ Jesus, in loving faithfulness to my countrymen's souls and defense of truth, I remember my worthy adversary of that state and condition from which his confessions say he must separate. His practice in gathering churches seems to say he doth separate; and yet he professeth there are but some remnants of pollution amongst them, for which he dare not separate. . . .

The close of his letter is an answer to a passage of mine . . . to which he answereth that they fear not the angel's curse because it is not to help Jehovah but Satan to withdraw people from the parishes where they have found more presence of Christ and evidence of His spirit than in separated churches; that they pray not for them because they cannot pray in faith for a blessing upon their separation; and that it is little comfort to hear of separate churches, as being inventions of men, and blames them that, being desirous of reformation, they stumble not only at the inventions of men but for their sakes at the ordinances of the Lord. . . .

Answer: However Mr. Cotton believes and writes of this point, yet hath he not duly considered these following particulars:

First, the faithful labors of many witnesses of Jesus Christ, extant to the world, abundantly proving that the church of the Jews under the Old Testament in the type and the church of the Christians under the New Testament in the antitype were both separate from the world; and that when they have opened a gap in the hedge or wall of separation between the garden of the church and the wilderness of the world, God hath ever broke down the wall itself, removed the candlestick, and made His garden a wilderness, as at this day. And that therefore if He will ever please to restore His garden and paradise again, it must of necessity be walled in peculiarly unto Himself from the world; and that all that shall be saved out of the world are to be transplanted out of the wilderness of the world, and added unto His church or garden.

Secondly, that all the grounds and principles leading to oppose bishops, ceremonies, Common Prayer, prostitution of the ordinances of Christ to the ungodly and to the true practice of Christ's own ordinances, do necessarily . . . conclude a separation of holy from unholy, penitent from impenitent, godly from ungodly; and that to frame any other building upon such grounds and foundations is no other than to raise the form of a square house upon the keel of a ship, which will never prove a soul-saving true ark or church of Christ Jesus according to the pattern.

Thirdly, the multitudes of holy and faithful men and women who, since Queen Mary's days, have witnessed this truth by writing, disputing, and in suffering loss of goods and friends, in imprisonments, banishments, death. I confess, the Nonconformists have suffered also: but they that have suffered for this cause have far exceeded, in not only witnessing to those grounds of the Nonconformists but to those truths also, the unavoidable conclusions of the Nonconformists' principles.

Fourthly, what is that which Mr. Cotton and so many hundreds fearing God in New England walk in but a way of separation? Of what matter do they profess to constitute their churches but of truly godly persons? In what form do they cast this matter but by a voluntary uniting or adding of such godly persons whom they carefully examine and cause to make a public confession of sin and profession of their knowledge and grace in Christ? Nay, when other English have attempted to set up a congregation after the parishional way, have they not been suppressed? Yea, have they not professedly and lately answered many worthy persons whom they account godly ministers and people that they could not permit them to live in the same commonwealth together with them if they set up any other church and worship than what themselves practice? . . .

Lastly, however, he saith he hath not found such presence of Christ and evidence of His spirit in such churches as in the parishes. What should be the reason of their great rejoicings and boastings of their own separations in New England, insomuch that some of the most eminent amongst them have affirmed that even the Apostles' churches were not so pure? Surely, if the same New English churches were in old England, they could not meet without persecution, which therefore in old England they avoid by frequenting the way of church worship which in New England they persecute, the parishes.

Upon these considerations, how can Mr. Cotton be offended that I should help (as he calls them) any zealous souls, not against the mighty ordinances of the Lord Jesus but to seek after the Lord Jesus without halting? Yea, why should Mr. Cotton or any desirous to practice reformation kindle a fire of persecution against such zealous souls, especially considering that themselves, had they so inveighed against bishops, Common Prayers, &c., in Edward VI his days, had been accounted as great heretics in those reforming times as any now can be in these? Yet would it have been then, and since hath it been, great oppression and tyranny to persecute their consciences, and still will it be for them to persecute the consciences of others in old and New England.

How can I better end than Mr. Cotton doth, by warning that all that will not kiss the Son (that is, hear and embrace the words of His mouth) shall perish in their way? And I desire Mr. Cotton and every soul to whom these lines may come seriously to consider, in this controversy, if the Lord Jesus were Himself in person in old or New England, what church, what ministry, what government He would set up, and what persecution He would practice toward them that would not receive Him?

III

On March 14, 1644, Parliament granted Rhode Island a charter, guaranteeing, as far as the Parliament could, independence and liberty of conscience. Williams might then have returned home, his mission accomplished and to his credit the first, as well as one of the most consummate, successes in American diplomacy. He stayed on, long enough to put through the press his masterpiece, the book which gives him his reputation with posterity, one of the greatest—if also one of the most gnarled and incoherent—utterances in the language: *The Bloudy Tenent, of Persecution, for cause of Conscience, discussed, in A Conference betweene Truth and Peace.*

It was released anonymously (but all England and soon all Protestantism knew the secret) on July 15, 1644, just as Williams was departing, armed with a Parliamentary safe-conduct which would oblige sullen Massachusetts to let him ashore in Boston. The book was hastily and spasmodically written; it was still more hastily printed. The first issue supplies a list of errata, some of which are corrected in the second, but even that is full of stupid errors. So muddled, so miserable is the printing that one wonders how, even in that day, any could follow the argument. Because it is a great work and cries out for liberation from its typography, I select and edit these magnificent pages.

The book is divided into two parts (the second from pages 118 to 247) because it addresses first Cotton's "Answer" to the Anabaptist tract, and then the ministerial *Model.* The first half confuses the reader because it is a three-level debate: the Anabaptist, who figures as the "Author," then Cotton, who is called the "Answerer," and finally "Peace" and "Truth," the protagonists of Williams, who descant on the other two and sometimes get so carried away by their eloquence as to lose sight of the sequence altogether.

Williams prefaces his dialogue with an address to Parliament—an act both of courage and foolhardiness, for Parliament was still dominated by Presbyterians. (Years later he said that the Presbyterians caused the book to be publicly burned, but confirming evidence hardly exists.) He artfully follows it with an address to "every courteous reader," knowing full well that by this time hundreds of Puritans, along with John Milton, were realizing that new presbyter was but old priest writ large. The immense buoyancy, the unflagging *élan*, flow from Williams' confidence that in his year abroad he had caught the drift of history. He was returning (voluntarily) to the wilderness, but by wilderness insights he had read aright the meaning of that civilized wilderness, the city of London. So, at the end of this oration, heaping up metaphors that defy punctuation, he composed his greatest paragraph, the living heart of his message (see page 111).

For the rest, the structure of the book is determined not by the logic of Williams' own thinking (we may well doubt that he could ever construct a sustained logical argument of his own, whereas in that very year Milton was composing sequential tracts on divorce—and *Aeropagitica*), but by point-to-point refutation of Cotton and of the *Model*. Since these gentlemen were trained logicians (so was Williams, but he could forget it), there is fortunately a certain progression, and because the *Model* necessarily concerned

itself with the church, Williams' book does come to a sort
of grand resolution in the typological vision. Yet Williams
does about all an author can do, by our standards, to spoil
his effects, blur his points, bury his finest passages in a
mass of haggling, and above all never let well enough alone.
That he should here have chosen the dialogue form shows
how much his emotionalism needed the release of the
dramatic form. For pages he not only immerses himself in
the most tedious of Biblical exegesis, but intersperses exposition with passionate addresses of Peace to Truth, or of
Truth to Peace, in which the limitations of his vocabulary
make for an eternal sameness. And throughout he shows
that trait which his letters also exhibit, such a lack of any
sense of proportion, not to mention elementary tact, that
every minor consideration is belabored with as much gusto
as a major topic. It is indeed miraculous—a tribute to the
passion which somehow did manage to get expressed—that
the book survives at all.

Cotton's "Answer" first laid down, in the manner of the
scholastic scholar, several "distinctions" about the nature
of conscience (Williams plays with these on page after
page), and then came resoundingly to the fundamental
thesis of Calvinist orthodoxy, a formulation which, we may
suggest, can be translated into other idiom and serve as the
basis for any sort of orthodoxy: the essentials of sound doctrine are so few, so clear, so simple, that any reasonable
man, having had them expounded to him by such a
"teacher" as Cotton, must be convinced of them; if he still
objects, and is once admonished, and then a second time
admonished, and still persists in error, he must be punished, because in this case "he is not persecuted for cause
of conscience, but for sinning against his own conscience."

The modern rejoinder, arising out of a conception of free competition among ideas, demands by what right Cotton sets himself up to determine the true conscience. How, we ask, does *he* know? Williams does come close to speaking thus, but seldom, and never in the tones of modern liberalism. For him the ideological issue is not central: the question is the meaning of Scripture. Were Cotton correct in saying that such-and-such is clearly demonstrable, Williams would have to agree that a good conscience ought to submit and allow the magistrate to help, just as we today believe that a judge can sentence unrepentant thieves. But the real problem, as Cotton made clear, resided in such important passages of the Bible as Matthew 13: 24-31, 37-43, in that puzzling business of the wheat and the tares. A master tells his servants not to pull up the tares lest they also root up the wheat; yet later, among the Disciples, Jesus predicts that at the end of the world, tares will be ruthlessly burned. Who, then, are these tares?

Cotton answered the conundrum in a way that made perfect sense within the dialectic of Nonseparation: the tares are hypocrites who manage to get into covenanted churches under a show of holiness, whom neither ministers nor congregations can detect. They must be let alone, to be judged on the Day of Doom. This argument was of great value to the New England Way because it proved to the world that, with all their noble aspirations, the colonists did not aim at an impossible perfection, that their idealism was practicable, that their revolutionary ardor was not visionary, that they knew a hawk from a handsaw. By claiming that their pure churches were not really pure, they could make them part of a civil order, of a functioning regime. If tares were the seemingly righteous *inside* the church, then heretics and disturbers of the theological peace *outside* the church could be pounced on by the civil government and mercilessly rooted up, without that agency being in the slightest degree guilty of "persecution."

To show how Williams' mind operated, I have given, along with his preliminary counterstatements, the substance of his section on the parable. His argument is that no church is so distinct from the wilderness of the world that in it, and in it alone, tares may be allowed to grow. Here is a good example of his method, but one can readily see that the thesis depends on a still anterior principle, the typological doctrine that emerges only at the end of his reply to the *Model*. In the remaining part of the attack on Cotton the more stirring passages also arise out of lengthy exegeses, but the modern reader's patience is short and space at a premium; I have therefore extracted sentences that can stand by themselves, although assuredly Williams would object to such surgery. Statements from Cotton or the *Model* figure, as generally they do in Williams, within quotation marks. As Williams, or his printer, prepared the book, there is a running commentary of marginal notes; mostly these are only subject headings, but where they clarify a point I have used them as statements of theme, or else relegated them according to modern usage to the footnotes.

The second portion, taking up the *Model*—after Peace and Truth have come to a rhapsodic paean over the corpse of Cotton—covers much the same ground, and in general is an anticlimax. However, the *Model* was explicitly di-

rected to the problem of church and state rather than to
the individual conscience. It too observed scholastic caution by marking off distinctions, and made full allowance
for the Puritan contention that the ecclesiastical and political spheres are separate. It declared that government
originates in the people (in accepting this premise Williams was no more "democratic" than his adversaries), and
that the people can choose what form of government they
wish (as Massachusetts under the charter had in effect
done).

But it then maintained that government, no matter what
the form, is to see that religion is not "corrupted." Therefore the magistrate must correct "delinquent" churches,
subdue obstreperous heretics and enforce the duties of
both Tables. He must punish gross and notorious sins
"against the light of conscience." Of course, the church
should first try to reform such culprits; but when it can
do no more, it must turn them over to the state. The
eleventh article, which catapulted Williams into open
avowal of typology, prevented the civil authority from de-
fining religious doctrine or telling ministers what to preach,
but demanded that he allow no freedom to any but sound
and solid congregations. "It is well known that remissness
in princes of Christendom in matters of religion and worship (devolving the care thereof only to the clergy, and
so setting the horns thereof upon the church's head) hath
been the cause of Antichristian inventions, usurpations and
corruptions in the worship and temple of God."

In short, the *Model* proposed that the state work on
churches exactly as Cotton called on it to deal with persons. To this pressure the congregation at Salem yielded

(all but a few, who followed Williams into the wilderness). But a church, in New England doctrine, was a covenanted society, "modeled" not only on the New but also on the Old Testament. Each society was a "little Israel." Therefore Williams was led by the *Model* to reveal his innermost idea, the insight that informs and directs all his uses of Scripture, most of all his handling of Matthew 13.

The crux of the difference is simple: the orthodox clergy distinguished between the realm of spirit and that of the body, and courageously said the two should not be confused. But then they said that when a church of covenanted saints misbehaves and resists the brotherly admonition of its neighbors, it can be treated by the authority of this world as no longer a body of dedicated spirits but as a disturber of the peace. The magistrates and their clerical friends decided that Salem was no longer a church but a mob. What, then, if this procedure be allowed, constitutes a church? Can there be such a thing?

Even if it were true, Williams tried to say, that his people, or any people anywhere, go so far astray that they are spiritually lost, they remain plants in the wilderness of the world. If they abide by the world's laws, no matter how much their opinions offend the dominant respectability, they are not to be bullied or bludgeoned into conformity. For where any longer is there a standard to which mankind must or can universally conform? The whole existing world, since the morning Christ ascended into heaven, is nothing but a wilderness; from that point of view there is little to choose, as to respectability and orthodoxy, as to spiritual truth, between the institutions of London or Boston and those of the barbarous Indians.

The Bloudy Tenent, of Persecution, for cause of
Conscience, discussed, in A Conference
betweene Truth and Peace

London, 1644

To the Right Honorable both Houses of the High Court of
Parliament
Right Honorable and Renowned Patriots:
NEXT TO saving of your own souls (in the lamentable shipwreck of mankind), your task as Christians is to save the souls, but as magistrates the bodies and goods of others.

Many excellent discourses have been presented to your fathers' hands and yours in former and present Parliaments: I shall be humbly bold to say that (in what concerns your duties as magistrates towards others) a more necessary and seasonable debate was never yet presented.

Two things your Honors here may please to view (in this controversy of persecution for cause of conscience) beyond what's extant:

First, the whole body of this controversy formed and pitched in true *battalia;*

Secondly, (although in respect of myself it be *impar congressus,* yet in the power of that God who is *maximus in minimis*) your Honors shall see the controversy is discussed with men as able as most, eminent for ability and piety, Mr. Cotton and the New English ministers. . . .

This glass presents your Honors with arguments from religion, reason, experience, all proving that the greatest yokes yet lying upon English necks (the people's and your own) are of a spiritual and soul nature.

All former Parliaments have changed these yokes according to their consciences (Popish or Protestant). 'Tis now your Honors' turn at helm, and as is your task so I hope is your resolution not to change (for that is but to turn the wheel which another Parliament, and the very next, may turn again) but to ease the subjects and yourselves from a yoke . . . which neither you nor your fathers were ever able to bear.

To every courteous reader:
WHILE I plead the cause of truth and innocency against the bloody doctrine of persecution for the cause of conscience, I judge it not unfit to give alarm to myself and all men to prepare to be persecuted or hunted for cause of conscience.

Whether thou standest charged with ten or but two talents, if thou huntest any for cause of conscience, how canst thou say thou followest the Lamb of God who so abhorred that practice?

If Paul, if Jesus Christ were present here at London, and the question were proposed what religion they would approve of—the Papists', Prelatists', Presbyterians', Independents'—would each say, "Of mine, of mine"?

But put the second question: if one of the several sorts should by major vote attain the sword of steel, what weapons doth Christ Jesus authorize them to fight with in His cause? Do not all men hate the persecutor, and every conscience, true or false, complain of cruelty, tyranny?

Two mountains of crying guilt lie heavy upon the backs of all that name the name of Christ in the eyes of Jews, Turks, and Pagans:

First, the blasphemies of their idolatrous inventions, superstitions, and most unchristian conversations;

Secondly, the bloody, irreligious, and inhumane oppressions and destructions under the mask or veil of the name of Christ. . . .

Who can now but expect that after so many scores of years' preaching and professing of more truth, and amongst so many great contentions amongst the very best of Protestants, a fiery furnace should be heated, and who sees not the fires kindling?

I confess I have little hopes till those flames are over that this discourse against the doctrine of persecution for cause of conscience should pass current (I say not amongst the wolves and lions but even amongst the sheep of Christ themselves). Yet *liberavi animam meam:* I have not hid within my breast my soul's belief. And although sleeping on the bed either of the pleasures or profits of sin, thou thinkest thy conscience bound to smite at him that dares to waken thee? Yet in the midst of all these civil and spiritual wars, I hope we shall agree in these particulars:

First, however the proud (upon the advantage of an higher earth or ground) o'erlook the poor and cry out, "Schismatics, heretics: shall blasphemers and seducers 'scape unpunished?" yet there is a sorer punishment in the Gospel for despising of Christ than Moses, even when the despiser of Moses was put to death without mercy: "he that believeth not shall be damned."

Secondly, whatever worship, ministry, ministration, the

best and purest practiced without faith and true persuasion that they are the true institutions of God, they are sin, sinful worships, ministries. And however in civil things we may be servants unto men, yet in divine and spiritual things the poorest peasant must disdain the service of the highest prince. . . .

Thirdly, without search and trial, no man attains this faith and right persuasion. . . .

In vain have English Parliaments permitted English Bibles in the poorest English houses, and the simplest man or woman to search the Scriptures, if yet against their souls' persuasion from the Scripture, they should be forced (as if they lived in Spain or Rome itself, without the sight of a Bible) to believe as the church believes.

Fourthly, having tried, we must hold fast, upon the loss of a crown; we must not let go for all the flea-bitings of the present afflictions. Having bought truth dear, we must not sell it cheap, not the least grain of it for the whole world, no, not for the saving of souls, though our own most precious. Least of all for the bitter sweetening of a little vanishing pleasure: for a little puff of credit and reputation from the changeable breath of uncertain sons of men: for the broken bags of riches on eagles' wings: for a dream of these, any or all these, which on our deathbed vanish and leave tormenting stings behind them. Oh, how much better is it from the love of truth, from the love of the Father of lights from whence it comes, from the love of the Son of God, who is the way and the truth, to say as He (John 18:37), "For this end was I born, and for this end came I into the world, that I might bear witness to the truth."

*A Reply to the aforesaid "Answer" of Mr. Cotton
In a Conference between Truth and Peace.*

Truth. In what dark corner of the world (sweet Peace)
are we two met? How hath this present evil world banished me from all the coasts and quarters of it? And how
hath the righteous God in judgment taken thee from the
earth?

Peace. 'Tis lamentably true (blessed Truth), the foundations of the world have long been out of course; the gates
of earth and hell have conspired together to intercept our
joyful meeting and our holy kisses. With what a wearied,
tired wing have I flown over nations, kingdoms, cities,
towns, to find out precious Truth?

Truth. The like inquiries in my flights and travels have
I made for Peace, and still am told, she hath left the earth
and fled to heaven.

Peace. Dear Truth, what is the earth but a dungeon of
darkness where truth is not?

Truth. And what's the peace thereof but a fleeting
dream, thine ape and counterfeit?

Peace. O, where's the promise of the God of Heaven,
that righteousness and peace shall kiss each other?

Truth. Patience (sweet Peace), these heavens and earth
are growing old, and shall be changed like a garment.
They shall melt away and be burned up with all the works
that are therein; and the most high eternal creator shall
glorious create new heavens and new earth, wherein
dwells righteousness. Our kisses then shall have their
endless date of pure and sweetest joys. Till then both thou
and I must hope and wait, and bear the fury of the dragon's

wrath, whose monstrous lies and furies shall with himself be cast into the lake of fire, the second death. . . .

Peace. O, how could I spend eternal days and endless dates at thy holy feet in listening to the precious oracles of thy mouth! All the words of thy mouth are truth, and there is no iniquity in them; thy lips drop as the honeycomb. But Oh! since we must part anon, let us (as thou saidest) improve our minutes, and (according as thou promisedst) revive me with thy words, which are sweeter than the honey and the honeycomb. . . .

Dear Truth, I have two sad complaints:

First, the most sober of thy witnesses that dare to plead thy cause, how are they charged to be mine enemies—contentious, turbulent, seditious?

Secondly, thine enemies, though they speak and rail against thee, though they outrageously pursue, imprison, vanish, kill thy faithful witnesses, yet how is all vermillioned o'er for justice 'gainst the heretics? Yea, if they kindle coals and blow the flames of devouring wars that leave neither spiritual nor civil state but burn up branch and root, yet how do all pretend an holy war? He that kills and he that's killed, they both cry out, it is for God and for their conscience. . . .

Truth. Sweet Peace, what hast thou there?

Peace. Arguments against persecution for cause of conscience.

Truth. And what there?

Peace. An "Answer" to such arguments, contrarily maintaining such persecution for cause of conscience.

Truth. These arguments against such persecution, and the "Answer" pleading for it, written (as love hopes) from godly intentions, hearts, and hands, yet in a marvelous different style and manner: the argument against persecution in milk, the "Answer" for it (as I may say) in blood. . . .

Peace. The "Answer" (though I hope out of milky pure intentions) is returned in blood: bloody and slaughterous conclusions, bloody to the souls of all men forced to the religion and worship which every civil state or commonweal agrees on and compels all subjects to in a dissembled uniformity.

Bloody to the bodies, first of the holy witnesses of Christ Jesus, who testify against such invented worships; secondly, of the nations and people slaughtering each other for their several respective religions and consciences. . . .

The first distinction is this: "By persecution for cause of conscience, I conceive you mean either for professing some point of doctrine which you believe in conscience to be the truth, or for practicing some work which you believe in conscience to be a religious duty."

Truth. . . . I desire it may be well observed that this distinction is not full and complete: for besides this, that a man may be persecuted because he holdeth or practiceth what he believes in conscience to be a truth. . . . I say besides this, a man may also be persecuted because he dares not be constrained to yield obedience to such doctrines and worships as are by men invented and appointed. . . . So thousands of Christ's witnesses (and of late in those bloody Marian days) have rather chose to yield their bodies to all sorts of torments than to subscribe to doctrines, or practice worships, unto which the states and times (as Nebuchadnezzar to his golden image) have compelled and urged them. . . .

Peace. The second distinction is this: "In points of doctrine, some are fundamental, without right belief whereof a man cannot be saved; others are circumstantial and less principal, wherein a man may differ in judgment without prejudice of salvation on either part."

Truth. To this distinction I dare not subscribe, for then I should everlastingly condemn thousands, and ten thousands, yea the whole generations of the righteous who since the falling away from the first primitive Christian state or worship have and do err fundamentally concerning the true matter, constitution, gathering, and governing of the church. And yet far be it from a pious breast to imagine that they are not saved and that their souls are not bound up in the bundle of eternal life.

We read of four sorts of spiritual or Christian foundations in the New Testament:

1. The foundation of all foundations, the cornerstone itself, the Lord Jesus, on whom all depend—persons, doctrine, practices.

2. Ministerial foundations. The church is built upon the foundation of the Apostles and Prophets.

3. The foundation of future rejoicing in the fruits of obedience.

4. The foundation of doctrines, without the knowledge of which there can be no true profession of Christ according to the first institution: the foundation or principles of repentance from dead works; faith towards God; the doctrine of baptism, laying on of hands, the resurrection, and eternal judgment. In some of these, to wit, those concerning baptism and laying on of hands, God's people will be found to be ignorant for many hundred years; and I yet cannot see it proved that light is risen, I mean the light of the first institution, in practice. . . .

If Mr. Cotton maintain the true church of Christ to consist of the true matter of holy persons called out from the world, and the true form of union in a church-covenant, and that also neither national, provincial, nor diocesan churches are of Christ's institution, how many thousands of God's people of all sorts (clergy and laity, as they call them) will they find, both in former and later times, captivated in such national, provincial, and diocesan churches? Yea, and so far from living in, yea or knowing of, any such churches (for matter and form) as they conceive now only to be true, that until of late years how few of God's people knew any other church than the parish church of dead stones or timber? ...

And however his own soul and the souls of many others (precious to God) are persuaded to separate from national, provincial, and diocesan churches, and to assemble into particular churches, yet since there are no parish churches in England but what are made up of the parish bounds, within such and such a compass of houses, and that such churches have been and are in constant dependence on, and subordination to, the national church: how can the New English particular churches join with the old English parish churches in so many ordinances of Word, prayer, singing, contribution, &c., but they must needs confess that as yet their souls are far from the knowledge of the foundation of a true Christian church, whose matter must not only be living stones but also separated from the rubbish of Antichristian confusions and desolations? ...

Peace. The next distinction concerning the manner of persons' holding forth the aforesaid practices (not only the weightier duties of the law but points of doctrine and worship less principal): "Some," saith he, "hold them forth in a meek and peaceable way; some with such arrogance and impetuousness as of itself tendeth to the disturbance of civil peace."

Truth. O, how lost are the sons of men in this point? To illustrate this: the church or company of worshippers (whether true or false) is like unto a body or college of physicians in a city; like unto a corporation, society, or company of East India or Turkey merchants, or any other society or company in London: which companies may hold their courts, keep their records, hold disputations, and in matters concerning their society may dissent, divide, break into schisms and factions, sue and implead each other at the law, yea, wholly break up and dissolve into pieces and nothing, and yet the peace of the city not be in the least measure impaired or disturbed. Because the essence or being of the city, and so the well-being and peace thereof, is essentially distinct from those particular societies; the city courts, city laws, city punishments distinct from theirs. The city was before them, and stands absolute and entire when such a corporation or society is taken down. . . .

Peace. Now to the second query: what it is to hold forth doctrine or practice in an arrogant or impetuous way?

Truth. Although it hath not pleased Mr. Cotton to declare what is this arrogant or impetuous holding forth of doctrine or practice tending to disturbance of civil peace, I cannot but express my sad and sorrowful observation how it pleaseth God to leave him, as to take up the common reproachful accusation of the accuser of God's children, to wit: that they are arrogant and impetuous, which charge (together with that of obstinacy, pertinacy, pride, troublers of the city, &c.) Satan commonly loads the meekest of the saints and witnesses of Jesus with. . . .

Peace. It will here be said, "Whence then ariseth civil dissensions and uproars about matters of religion?"

Truth. I answer: when a kingdom or state, town or

family, lies and lives in the guilt of a false God, false Christ, false worship, no wonder if sore eyes be troubled at the appearance of the light, be it never so sweet? No wonder if a body full of corrupt humors be troubled at strong (though wholesome) physic? If persons sleepy and loving to sleep be troubled at the noise of shrill (though silver) alarms, no wonder if Adonijah and all his company be amazed and troubled at the sound of the right heir, King Solomon? If the husbandmen were troubled when the Lord of the vineyard sent servant after servant, and at last His only Son, and they beat and wounded and killed even the Son Himself, because they meant themselves to seize upon the inheritance unto which they had no right? Hence all those tumults about the Apostles in the Acts, whereas good eyes are not so troubled at light; vigilant and watchful persons, loyal and faithful, are not so troubled at the true, no, nor at a false religion of Jew or Gentile.

Secondly, breach of civil peace may arise when false and idolatrous practices are held forth, and yet no breach of civil peace from the doctrine or practice or the manner of holding forth, but from that wrong and preposterous way of suppressing, preventing, and extinguishing such doctrines or practices by weapons of wrath and blood—whips, stocks, imprisonment, banishment, death, &c.—by which men commonly are persuaded to convert heretics and to cast out unclean spirits, which only the finger of God can do, that is, the mighty power of the Spirit in the Word.

Hence the town is in an uproar and the country takes the alarm to expel that fog or mist of error, heresy, blasphemy (as is supposed) with swords and guns; whereas 'tis light alone, even light from the bright shining sun of righteousness, which is able, in the souls and consciences of men, to dispel and scatter such fogs and darkness. . . .

Peace. Now the last distinction is this: "Persecution for conscience is either for a rightly informed conscience, or a blind and erroneous conscience."

Truth. Indeed, both these consciences are persecuted. But lamentably blind and erroneous will these consciences shortly appear to be which, out of zeal for God (as is pretended), have persecuted either. And heavy is the doom of those blind guides and idol shepherds (whose right eye God's finger of jealousy hath put out) who, flattering the ten horns or worldly powers, persuade them what excellent and faithful service they perform to God in persecuting both these consciences: either hanging up a rightly informed conscience, and therein the Lord Jesus Himself, between two malefactors, or else killing the erroneous and the blind, like Saul (out of zeal to the Israel of God) the poor Gibeonites whom it pleased God to permit to live. And yet that hostility and cruelty used against them (as the repeated judgment, year after year, upon the whole land often told them) could not be pardoned until the death of the persecutor Saul, and his sons had appeased the Lord's displeasure. . . .

Peace. He holds it not lawful to persecute any for conscience sake rightly informed: "For in persecuting such," saith he, "Christ Himself is persecuted." . . .

Truth. He that shall read this conclusion over a thousand times shall as soon find darkness in the bright beams of the sun as in this so clear and shining beam of truth, *viz.*, that Christ Jesus in His truth must not be persecuted.

Yet this I must ask (for it will be admired by all sober men), what should be the cause or inducement to the Answerer's mind to lay down such a position or thesis as this is, "It is not lawful to persecute the Lord Jesus"?

Search all Scriptures, histories, records, monuments—consult with all experiences—did ever Pharaoh, Saul, Ahab, Jezebel, Scribes and Pharisees, the Jews, Herod, the bloody Neros, Gardiners[7], Bonners[8], pope or devil himself, profess to persecute the Son of God, Jesus as Jesus, Christ as Christ, without a mask or covering?

No, saith Pharaoh, the Israelites are idle, and therefore speak they of sacrificing; David is risen up in a conspiracy against Saul, therefore persecute him; Naboth hath blasphemed God and the king, therefore stone him; Christ is a seducer of the people, a blasphemer against God and traitor against Caesar, therefore hang Him; Christians are schismatical, factious, heretical, therefore persecute them; the Devil hath deluded John Huss, therefore crown him with a paper of devils and burn him. . . .

Peace. Their second conclusion is this: . . . "The Word of God is so clear in fundamental and weighty points that such a person cannot but sin against his conscience, and so being condemned of himself—that is, his conscience—he may be persecuted for sinning against his own conscience." . . .

Truth. Of this reason, I find not one tittle mentioned in this Scripture; for although he [Paul] saith such an one is condemned of himself, yet he saith not, nor will it follow, that fundamentals are so clear that after first and second admonition a person that submits not to them is condemned of himself. . . .

Concerning these fundamentals (although nothing is so little in the Christian worship but may be referred to one of these six,[9] yet) doth not Paul to Timothy or Titus speak in those places by me alleged, or of any of these, as may evidently appear by the context and scope?

The beloved spouse of Christ is no receptacle for any filthy person obstinate in any filthiness against the purity of the Lord Jesus, who hath commanded His people to purge out the old leaven, not only greater portions but a little leaven which will leaven the whole lump; and therefore this heretic or obstinate person in these vain and unprofitable questions was to be rejected, as if his obstinacy had been in greater matters.

Again, if there were a door or window left open to vain and unprofitable questions and sins of smaller nature, how apt are persons to cover with a silken covering, and to say, "Why, I am no heretic in fundamentals, spare me in this or that little one, this or that opinion or practice, these are of an inferior, circumstantial nature."

So that the coherence with the former verses, and the scope of the Spirit of God in this and other like Scriptures being carefully observed, this Greek word "heretic" is no more in true English and in truth than an obstinate or wilful person in the church of Crete striving and contending about those unprofitable questions and genealogies, &c., and is not such a monster intended in this place, as most interpreters run upon: to wit, one obstinate in fundamentals.

[Williams' examination of Matthew 13, the parable of the wheat and the tares.]

Peace. We are now come to the second part of the "Answer," which is a particular examination of such grounds as are brought against such persecution.

First, Matthew 13, because Christ commandeth to let alone the tares to grow up together with the wheat until the harvest.

Unto which he answereth: that tares are not briars and thorns, but partly hypocrites, like unto the godly but indeed carnal (as the tares are like to wheat but are not wheat), or partly such corrupt doctrines and practices as are indeed unsound but yet such as come very near the truth (as tares do to the wheat) and so near that good men may be taken with them; and so the persons in whom they grow cannot be rooted out but good wheat will be rooted out with them. "In such a case," saith he, "Christ calleth for peaceable toleration and not for penal prosecution."

Truth. The substance of this answer I conceive to be first negative: that by tares are not meant persons of another religion and worship; that is, he saith, they are not briars and thorns.

Secondly, affirmative: by tares are meant either persons, or doctrines, or practices: persons, as hypocrites like the godly; doctrines or practices corrupt, yet like the truth.

But alas! how dark is the soul left that desires to walk with God in holy fear and trembling, when in such a weighty and mighty point as this is—that in matters of conscience concerning the spilling of the blood of thousands and the civil peace of the world, in taking up arms to suppress all false religions—when, I say, no evidence or demonstration of the Spirit is brought to prove such an interpretation, nor arguments from the place itself or the Scriptures of truth to confirm it, but a bare affirmation that these tares must signify persons, or doctrines and practices! . . .

Peace. The place then being of such great importance as concerning the truth of God, the blood of thousands—yea, the blood of saints and of the Lord Jesus in them—I shall request your more diligent search (by the Lord's holy assistance) into this Scripture.

Truth. I shall make it evident that by these tares in this parable are meant persons in respect of their religion and way of worship—open and visible professors, as bad as briars and thorns—not only suspected foxes, but as bad as those greedy wolves which Paul speaks of (Acts 20) who, with perverse and evil doctrines, labor spiritually to devour the flock and to draw away disciples after them, whose mouths must be stopped and yet no carnal force or weapon be used against them: but their mischief to be resisted with those mighty weapons of the holy armory of the Lord Jesus, wherein there hang a thousand shields. . . .

Hypocrites were not intended by the Lord Jesus in this famous parable. . . . When was it that the householder gave charge to let them alone, but after they appeared and were known to be tares? Which should imply, by this interpretation of the Answerer, that when men are discovered and known to be hypocrites, yet still such a generation of hypocrites in the church must be let alone and tolerated until the harvest or end of the world—which is contrary to all order, piety, and safety in the church of the Lord Jesus, as doubtless the Answerer will grant. So that, these tares being notoriously known to be different from the corn, I conclude that they cannot here be intended by the Lord Jesus to signify secret hypocrites but more open and apparent sinners.

The second reason why these tares cannot signify hypocrites in the church, I take from the Lord Jesus His own interpretation of the "field" (in which both wheat and tares are sown), which, saith He, is the world, out of which God chooseth and calleth His church.

The world lies in wickedness, is like a wilderness or a sea of wild beasts innumerable—fornicators, covetous, idolaters, &c., &c.—with whom God's people may lawfully converse and cohabit in cities, towns, &c., else must they not live in the world but go out of it. In which world—as soon as ever the Lord Jesus had sown the good seed, the children of the kingdom, true Christianity or the true church—the enemy Satan, presently in the night of security, ignorance, and error (whilst men slept), sowed also these tares, which are Antichristians or false Christians. These strange professors of the name of Jesus, the ministers and prophets of God beholding, they are ready to run to heaven to fetch fiery judgments from thence to consume these strange Christians, and to pluck them by the roots out of the world. But the Son of Man, the meek Lamb of God (for the elects' sake, which must be gathered out of Jew and Gentile, pagan, antichristian) commands a permission of them in the world until the time of the end of the world, when the goats and sheep, the tares and wheat, shall be eternally separated each from other. . . .

In the former parable, the Lord Jesus compared the kingdom of heaven to the sowing of seed. The true messengers of Christ are the sowers, who cast the seed of the Word of the kingdom upon four sorts of ground, which four sorts of ground or hearts of men cannot be supposed to be of the church; nor will it ever be proved that the church consisteth of any more sorts or natures of ground, properly, but one—to wit, the honest and good ground. And the proper work of the church concerns the flourishing and prosperity of this sort of ground, and not the other unconverted three sorts, who it may be seldom or never come near the church unless they be forced by the civil sword (which the pattern or first sowers never used), and being forced, they are put into a way of religion by such a course. If not so, they are forced to live without a religion, for one of the two must necessarily follow. . . .

Now, after the Lord Jesus had propounded that great leading parable of the sower and the seed, He is pleased to propound this parable of the tares, with admirable coherence and sweet consolation to the honest and good ground, who with glad and honest hearts, having received the Word of the kingdom, may yet seem to be discouraged and troubled with so many antichristians and false professors of the name of Christ. The Lord Jesus therefore gives direction concerning these tares, that unto the end of the world, successively in all the sorts and generations of them, they must be (not approved or countenanced, but) let alone or permitted in the world.

Secondly, he gives to His own good seed this consolation, that those heavenly reapers, the angels in the harvest or end of the world, will take an order and course with them: to wit, they shall bind them into bundles and cast them into everlasting burnings. . . .

Peace. Oh, how contrary unto this command of the Lord Jesus have such as have conceived themselves the true messengers of the Lord Jesus in all ages not let such professors and prophets alone, whom they have judged tares, but have provoked kings and kingdoms (and some out of good intentions and zeal to God) to prosecute and persecute such even unto death? Amongst whom, God's people (the good wheat) hath also been plucked up, as all ages and histories testify; and, too, too oft the world laid upon bloody heaps in civil and intestine desolations on this occasion. All which would be prevented—and the greatest breaches made up in the peace of our own or other countries—were this command of the Lord Jesus obeyed: to wit, to let them alone until the harvest. . . .

And therefore I conclude, it was in one respect that the Lord Jesus said, "Let them alone," because it was no ordinance for any disciple of Jesus to prosecute the Pharisees at Caesar's bar.

Besides, let it be seriously considered by such as plead for present corporal punishment—as conceiving that such sinners (though they break not civil peace) should not escape unpunished—I say, let it be considered, though for the present their punishment is deferred, yet the punishment inflicted on them will be found to amount to an higher pitch than any corporal punishment in the world besides. . . .

Peace. Some will say these things are indeed full of horror, yet such is the state of all sinners and of many malefactors whom yet the state is bound to punish, and sometimes by death itself.

Truth. I answer, the civil magistrate beareth not the sword in vain, but to cut off civil offenses, yea, and the offenders, too, in case. But what is this to a blind Pharisee resisting the doctrine of Christ who happily may be as good a subject, and as peaceable and profitable to the civil state, as any: and for his spiritual offense against the Lord Jesus, in denying Him to be the true Christ, he suffereth the vengeance of a dreadful judgment both present and eternal?

Peace. Yea, but it is said that the blind Pharisee's misguiding the subjects of a civil state greatly sin against a civil state, and therefore justly suffer civil punishment; for shall the civil magistrate take care of outsides only, to wit, the bodies of men, and not of souls, in laboring to procure their everlasting welfare?

Truth. I answer, it is a truth, the mischief of a blind Pharisee's blind guidance is greater than if he acted treasons, murders, &c., and the loss of one soul by his seduction is a greater mischief than if he blew up Parliaments and cut the throats of kings or emperors, so precious is that invaluable jewel of a soul, above all the present lives and bodies of all the men in the world! And therefore a firm justice, calling for eye for eye, tooth for tooth, life for life, calls also soul for soul—which the blind-guiding, seducing Pharisee shall surely pay in that dreadful ditch which the Lord Jesus speaks of. But this sentence against him, the Lord Jesus only pronounceth in His church, His spiritual judicature, and executes this sentence in part at present and hereafter to all eternity. Such a sentence no civil judge can pass, such a death no civil sword can inflict.[10]

I answer secondly, dead men cannot be infected. The civil state, the world, being in a natural state dead in sin (whatever be the state religion unto which persons are forced), it is impossible it should be infected. Indeed, the living, the believing, the church and spiritual state, that and that only is capable of infection, for whose help we shall presently see what preservatives and remedies the Lord Jesus hath appointed.

Moreover, as we see in a common plague or infection, the names are taken how many are to die, and not one more shall be struck than the destroying angel hath the names of. So here, whatever be the soul-infection breathed out

from the lying lips of a plague-sick Pharisee, yet the names
are taken; not one elect or chosen of God shall perish,
God's sheep are safe in His eternal hand and counsel, and
He that knows His material knows also His mystical stars,
their number, and calls them every one by name. None
fall into the ditch on the blind Pharisee's back but such as
were ordained to that condemnation, both guide and followers.

Truth. I observe that he [Cotton] implies that beside
the censure of the Lord Jesus, in the hands of His spiritual
governors, for any spiritual evil in life or doctrine, the
civil magistrate is also to inflict corporal punishment upon
the contrary minded. Whereas,

First, if the civil magistrate be a Christian, a disciple or
follower of the meek Lamb of God, he is bound to be far
from destroying the bodies of men for refusing to receive
the Lord Jesus Christ, for otherwise he should not know
(according to this speech of the Lord Jesus) what spirit
he was of—yea, and to be ignorant of the sweet end of the
coming of the Son of Man, which was not to destroy the
bodies of men, but to save both bodies and souls.

Secondly, if the civil magistrate, being a Christian,
gifted, prophesy in the church, although the Lord Jesus
Christ, whom they in their own persons hold forth, shall
be refused, yet they are here forbidden to call for fire from
heaven—that is, to procure or inflict any corporal judgment
upon such offenders, remembering the end of the Lord
Jesus His coming, not to destroy men's lives but to save
them.

Lastly, this also concerns the conscience of the civil

magistrate: as he is bound to preserve the civil peace and quiet of the place and people under him, he is bound to suffer no man to break the civil peace by laying hands of violence upon any, though as vile as the Samaritans for not receiving of the Lord Jesus Christ.

It is indeed the ignorance and blind zeal of the second beast, the false prophet, to persuade the civil powers of the earth to persecute the saints—that is, to bring fiery judgments upon men in a judicial way, and to pronounce that such judgments of imprisonment, banishment, death proceed from God's righteous vengeance upon such heretics. So dealt divers bishops in France, and England, too, in Queen Mary's days, with the saints of God at their putting them to death, declaiming against them in their sermons to the people and proclaiming that these persecutions even unto death were God's "just judgments from heaven upon these heretics."

(Patience and meekness required in all that open Christ's mysteries.) [Williams' marginal note.]

Truth. I argue from this place of Timothy[11] in particular, thus:

First, if the civil magistrates be Christians or members of the church, able to prophesy in the church of Christ, then I say as before, they are bound by this command of Christ to suffer opposition to their doctrine with meekness and gentleness, and to be so far from striving to subdue their opposites with the civil sword that they are bound with patience and meekness to wait if God peradventure will please to grant repentance unto their opposites.

So also it pleaseth the Answerer to acknowledge in these

words: "It becomes not the Spirit of the Gospel to convert aliens to the faith (such as the Samaritans and the unconverted Christians in Crete) with fire and brimstone."

Secondly, be they oppositions within, and church members (as the Answerer speaks) become scandalous in doctrine (I speak not of scandal against the civil state, which the civil magistrate ought to punish), it is the Lord only who is able to give them repentance and recover them out of Satan's snare: to which end also He hath appointed those holy and dreadful censures in His church or kingdom. True it is, the sword may make a whole nation of hypocrites. But to recover a soul from Satan by repentance, and to bring them from antichristian doctrine or worship to the doctrine or worship Christian, in the least true internal or external submission, that only works the all-powerful God by the sword of the Spirit in the hand of His spiritual officers.

What a most woeful proof hereof have the nations of the earth given in all ages? And to seek no further than our native soil, within a few score of years how many wonderful changes in religion hath the whole kingdom made, according to the change of the governors thereof, in the several religions which they themselves embraced! Henry VII finds and leaves the kingdom absolutely Popish. Henry VIII casts it into a mold half-Popish, half-Protestant. Edward VI brings forth an edition all Protestant. Queen Mary within a few years defaceth Edward's work and renders the kingdom (after her grandfather Henry VII his pattern) all Popish. Mary's short life and religion end together; and Elizabeth reviveth her brother Edward's model, all Protestant. And some eminent witnesses of God's truth against Antichrist have inclined to believe that before the downfall of that beast, England must once again bow down her fair neck to his proud, usurping yoke and foot.

Peace. It hath been England's sinful shame to fashion and change their garments and religions with wondrous ease and lightness, as a higher power, a stronger sword, hath prevailed; after the ancient pattern of Nebuchadnezzar's bowing the whole world in one most solemn uniformity of worship to his golden image.

Truth. To keep to the similitude which the Spirit useth—for instance, to batter down a stronghold, high wall, fort, tower, or castle, men bring not a first and second admonition, and after obstinacy, excommunication—which are spiritual weapons concerning them that be in the church—nor exhortation to repent and be baptized, to believe in the Lord Jesus—which are proper weapons to them that be without. But to take a stronghold, men bring cannons, culverins, sakers,[12] bullets, powder, muskets, swords, pikes; and these to this end are weapons effectual and proportionable.

On the other side, to batter down idolatry, false worship, heresy, schism, blindness, hardness, out of the soul and spirit, it is vain, improper, and unsuitable to bring those weapons which are used by persecutors—stocks, whips, prisons, swords, gibbets, stakes (where these seem to prevail with some cities or kingdoms, a stronger force sets up again what a weaker pulled down)—but against these spiritual strongholds in the souls of men, spiritual artillery and weapons are proper, which are mighty through God to subdue and bring under the very thought to obedience, or else to bind fast the soul with chains of darkness and lock it up in the prison of unbelief and hardness to eternity.

I observe that as civil weapons are improper in this business, and never able to effect aught in the soul, so (although they were proper, yet) they are unnecessary: for if as the Spirit here saith (and the Answerer grants) spiritual weapons in the hand of church officers are able and ready to take vengeance on all disobedience, that is able and mighty, sufficient and ready, for the Lord's work—either to save the soul or to kill the soul of whomsoever be the party or parties opposite, in which respect I may again remember that speech of Job: "How hast thou helped him that hath no power?"

Peace. Offer this (as Malachi once spake) to the governors, the kings of the earth: when they besiege, beleaguer, and assault great cities, castles, forts, should any subject pretending his service bring store of pins, sticks, straws, bulrushes, to beat and batter down stone walls, mighty bulwarks, what might his expectation and reward be but at least the censure of a man distract, beside himself? . . .

Truth. Will the Lord Jesus (did He ever in His own person practice, or did he appoint to) join to His breastplate of righteousness the breastplate of iron and steel? To the helmet of righteousness and salvation in Christ, an helmet and crest of iron, brass, or steel, a target of wood to His shield of faith? To His two-edged sword, coming forth of the mouth of Jesus, the material sword, the work of smith's girdle and cutler's? Or a girdle of shoe's leather to the girdle of truth? Excellently fit and proper is that alarm and item (Psalms 2): Be wise, therefore, O ye kings, who under pretense of fighting for Christ Jesus give their power to the beast against Him, and be warned, ye judges of the earth: kiss the Son. That is, with subjection and affection, acknowledge Him only the King and Judge of souls (in that power bequeathed to His ministers and churches), lest if His wrath be kindled, yea but a little, then blessed are they that trust in Him.

Truth. There is a civil sword, called the sword of civil justice, which, being of a material civil nature, for the defense of persons, estates, families, liberties of a city or civil state, and the suppressing of uncivil or injurious persons or actions by such civil punishments—it cannot, according to its utmost reach and capacity (now under Christ, when all nations are merely civil, without any such typical, holy respect upon them as was upon Israel, a national church), I say, cannot extend to spiritual and soul causes, spiritual and soul punishment, which belongs to that spiritual sword with two edges, the soul-piercing (in soul-saving or soul-killing), the Word of God.

(Evil is always evil, yet permission of it may in case be good.) [Williams' marginal note.]

Truth. It must be remembered that it is one thing to command, to conceal, to counsel, to approve evil; and another thing to permit and suffer evil with protestation against it or dislike of it, at least without approbation of it.

This sufferance or permission of evil is not for its own sake but for the sake of good, which puts a respect of goodness upon such permission.

Hence it is that for God's own glory sake (which is the

highest good) He endures—that is, permits or suffers—the
vessels of wrath. And therefore, although He be of pure
eyes and can behold no iniquity, yet His pure eyes patiently and quietly behold and permit all the idolatries and
profanations, all the thefts and rapines, all the whoredoms
and abominations, all the murders and poisonings: and yet,
I say, for His glory sake He is patient and long permits. . . .

Therefore He would not so soon have destroyed Sodom
but granted a longer permission had there been but ten
righteous. . . .

Therefore for His glory sake hath He permitted longer
great sinners, who afterward have perished in their season,
as we see in the case of Ahab, the Ninevites, and Amorites.

Hence it pleased the Lord not only to permit the many
evils against His own honorable ordinance of marriage in
the world, but He was pleased after a wonderful manner
to suffer that sin of many wives in Abraham, Jacob, David,
Solomon, yea, with some expressions which seem to give
approbation.

Peace. It may be said this is no pattern for us, because
God is above the law and an absolute sovereign.

Truth. I answer, although we find Him sometime dis-
pensing with His law, yet we never find Him deny Himself or utter a falsehood. And therefore, when it crosseth
not an absolute rule to permit and tolerate (as in the case
of the permission of the souls and consciences of all men
in the world), it will not hinder our being holy as He is
holy in all manner of conversation.

Truth. All may see how, since the apostasy of Antichrist, the Christian world (so-called) hath swallowed up

Christianity, how the church and civil state—that is, the church and world—are now become one flock of Jesus Christ: Christ's sheep and the pastors or shepherds of them all one with the several unconverted, wild or tame beasts and cattle of the world, and the civil and earthly governors of them; the Christian church or kingdom of the saints, that stone cut out of the mountain without hands, now made all one with the mountain or civil state, the Roman Empire, from whence it is cut or taken; Christ's lilies, garden, and love, all one with the thorns, the daughters and wilderness of the world, out of which the spouse or church of Christ is called, and amongst whom in civil things for a while here below she must necessarily be mingled and have converse, unless she will go out of the World (before Christ Jesus, her Lord and Husband, send for her home into the heavens).[13]

Truth. I affirm that that state policy and state necessity which (for the peace of the state and preventing of rivers of civil blood) permits the consciences of men will be found to agree most punctually with the rules of the best politician that ever the world saw, the King of kings and Lord of lords, in comparison of whom Solomon himself had but a drop of wisdom, compared to Christ's ocean, and was but a farthing candle compared with the all and ever glorious Son of righteousness.

Truth. Precious pearls and jewels, and far more precious truth, are found in muddy shells and places. The rich mines of golden truth lie hid under barren hills and in obscure holes and corners.

The most high and glorious God hath chosen the poor of the world; and the witnesses of truth are clothed in sackcloth, not in silk or satin, cloth of gold or tissue. And therefore I acknowledge, if the number of princes professing persecution be considered, it is rare to find a king, prince, or governor like Christ Jesus, the King of kings and Prince of the princes of earth, and who treads not in the steps of Herod the Fox or Nero the Lion, openly or secretly persecuting the name of the Lord Jesus. Such were Saul, Jeroboam, Ahab, though under a mask or pretense of the name of the God of Israel.

To that purpose was it a noble speech of Buchanan,[14] who, lying on his deathbed, sent this item to King James: "Remember my humble service to His Majesty, and tell him that Buchanan is going to a place where few kings come."

Peace. I have often heard that history reports, and I have heard that Mr. Cotton himself hath affirmed it, that Christianity fell asleep in Constantine's bosom and the laps and bosoms of those emperors professing the name of Christ.

Truth. The unknowing zeal of Constantine and other emperors did more hurt to Christ Jesus His crown and kingdom than the raging fury of the most bloody Neros. In the persecutions of the latter, Christians were sweet and fragrant, like spice pounded and beaten in mortars; but those good emperors, persecuting some erroneous persons— Arius, &c.—and advancing the professors of some truths of Christ (for there was no small number of truths lost in those times) and maintaining their religion by the material sword—I say, by this means Christianity was eclipsed and the professors of it fell asleep. Babel or confusion was ushered in, and by degrees the garden of the churches of saints were turned into the wilderness of whole nations, until the whole world became Christian or Christendom.

Doubtless those holy men, emperors and bishops, intended and aimed right, to exalt Christ: but not attending to the command of Christ Jesus to permit the tares to grow in the field of the world, they made the garden of the church and field of the world to be all one; and might not only sometimes in their zealous mistakes persecute good wheat instead of tares, but also pluck up thousands of those precious stalks by commotions and combustions about religion, as hath been since practiced in the great and wonderful changes wrought by such wars in many great and mighty states and kingdoms. . . .

Oh, it is hard for God's children to fall to opinion and practice of persecution without the ready learning the language thereof: and doubtless that soul that can so readily speak Babel's language hath cause to fear that he hath not yet in point of worship left the gates or suburbs of it. . . .

If the weeds be kept out of the garden of the church, the roses and lilies therein will flourish, notwithstanding that weeds abound in the field of the civil state. When Christianity began to be choked, it was not when Christians lodged in cold prisons, but down-beds of ease.

Peace. He [Cotton] ends this passage with approbation of Queen Elizabeth for persecuting the Papists, and a reproof to King James for his persecuting the Puritans.

Truth. I answer, if Queen Elizabeth, according to the

Answerer's tenent and conscience, did well to persecute according to her conscience, King James did not ill in persecuting according to his. For Mr. Cotton must grant that either King James was not fit to be a king, had not the essential qualifications of a king, in not being able rightly to judge who ought to be persecuted and who not; or else he must confess that King James and all magistrates must persecute such whom in their conscience they judge worthy to be persecuted.

I say it again, (though I neither approve Queen Elizabeth or King James in such their persecutions, yet) such as hold this tenent of persecuting for conscience must also hold that civil magistrates are not essentially fitted and qualified for their function and office except they can discern clearly the difference between such as are to be punished and persecuted and such as are not.

Or else, if they be essentially qualified without such a religious spirit of discerning, and yet must persecute the heretic, the schismatic, must they not persecute according to their conscience and persuasion? And then, doubtless, (though he be excellent for civil government) may he easily, as Paul did ignorantly, persecute the Son of God instead of the son of perdition.

Truth. The civil state and magistracy judging in spiritual things: who knows not what constraint lies upon all consciences in old and New England to come to church and pay church duties, which is upon the point (though with a sword of a finer gilt and trim in New England) nothing else but that which he [Cotton] confesseth Hilary saith true should not be done—to wit, a propagation of religion by the sword. Again, although he confesseth that propagation of religion ought not to be by the sword, yet he maintaineth the use of the sword when persons (in the judgment of the civil state, for that is implied) blaspheme the true God and the true religion, and also seduce others to damnable heresy and idolatry.

Truth. In New England, it is well known that they not only permit the Indians to continue in their unbelief (which neither they nor all the ministers of Christ on earth nor angels in heaven can help, not being able to work belief), but they also permit or tolerate them in their paganish worship, which cannot be denied to be a worshipping of devils, as all false worship is.

And therefore consequently, according to the same practice, did they walk by rule and impartiality, not only the Indians but their countrymen, French, Dutch, Spanish, Persians, Turks, Jews, should also be permitted in their worships if correspondent in civil obedience. . . .

First, a false religion out of the church will not hurt the church, no more than weeds in the wilderness hurt the enclosed garden, or poison hurt the body when it is not touched or taken, yea, and antidotes are received against it.

Secondly, a false religion and worship will not hurt the civil state in case the worshipper break no civil law. And the Answerer acknowledgeth that the civil laws not being broken, civil peace is not broken: and this only is the point in question.

Peace. The next passage in the Author which the Answerer descends unto is the testimony of the Papists them-

selves, a lively and shining testimony from Scriptures
alleged both against themselves and all that associate with
them (as power is in their hand) in such unchristian and
bloody both tenents and practices:

"As for the testimony of the Popish book," saith he, "we
weigh it not, as knowing whatever they speak for toleration of religion where themselves are under hatches, when
they come to sit at stern they judge and practice quite contrary, as both their writings and judicial proceedings have
testified to the world these many years."

Truth. I answer: although both writings and practices
have been such, yet the Scriptures and expressions of truth
alleged and uttered by them speak loud, and fully, for them
when they are under the hatches, that for their conscience
and religion they should not there be choked and smoth-
ered, but suffered to breathe and walk upon the decks in
the air of civil liberty and conversation in the ship of the
commonwealth, upon good assurance given of civil obedience to the civil state.

Again, if this practice be so abominable in his eyes from
the Papists, *viz.*, that they are so partial as to persecute
when they sit at helm, and yet cry out against persecution
when they are under the hatches, I shall beseech the
righteous judge of the whole world to present as in a water
or glass (where face answereth to face) the faces of the
Papist to the Protestant, answering to each other in the
sameness of partiality, both of this doctrine and practice.

When Mr. Cotton and others have formerly been under
hatches, what sad and true complaints have they abundantly poured forth against persecution? . . . But coming
to the helm (as he speaks of the Papists), how, both by
preaching, writing, printing, practice, do they themselves

(I hope in their persons lambs) unnaturally and partially express toward others the cruel nature of such lions and leopards?

O, that the God of heaven might please to tell them how abominable in His eyes are a weight and a weight, a stone and a stone, in the bag of weights! One weight for themselves when they are under hatches, and another for others when they come to helm.

Nor shall their confidence of their being in the truth (which they judge the Papists and others are not in), no, nor the truth itself, privilege them to persecute others and to exempt themselves from persecution. . . .

Notwithstanding their confidence of the truth of their own way, yet the experience of our fathers' errors, our own mistakes and ignorance, the sense of our own weaknesses and blindness in the depths of the prophecies and mysteries of the kingdom of Christ, and the great professed expectation of light to come which we are not now able to comprehend, may abate the edge, yea, sheath up the sword of persecution toward any, especially such as differ not from them in doctrines of repentance, or faith, or holiness of heart and life, and hope of glorious and eternal union to come, but only in the way and manner of the administrations of Jesus Christ.

Peace. Yes, but they [the New England clergy] say, "We are but weak men and dream not of perfection in this life."

Truth. Alas! who knows not what lamentable differences have been between the same ministers of the Church of England: some conforming, others leaving their livings,

friends, country, life rather than conform, when others
again (of whose personal godliness it is not questioned)
have succeeded by conformity into such forsaken (so-
called) livings? How great the present differences even
amongst them that fear God concerning faith, justification
and the evidence of it, concerning repentance and godly
sorrow, as also and mainly concerning the church—the
matter, form, administrations, and government of it?

Let none now think that the passage to New England
by sea, nor the nature of the country, can do what only the
key of David can do—to wit, open and shut the consciences
of men.

Besides, how can this be a faithful and upright acknowledgment of their weakness and imperfection when they
preach, print, and practice such violence to the souls and
bodies of others, and by their rules and grounds ought to
proceed even to the killing of those whom they judge so
dear unto them—and in respect of godliness far above
themselves?

Peace. "Yea, but," say they, "the godly will not persist
in heresy or turbulent schism when they are convinced in
conscience."

Truth. According to this conclusion it must follow that
if the most godly persons yield not to once or twice admonition (as is maintained by the Answerer) they must
necessarily be esteemed obstinate persons, for if they were
godly (saith he) they would yield. Must it not then be
said (as it was by one passing sentence of banishment upon
one whose godliness was acknowledged) that He that
commanded the judge not to respect the poor in cause of
judgments commands him not to respect the holy or the
godly person? . . .

Peace. Mr. Cotton concludes with a confident persuasion of having removed the grounds of that great error, *viz.*, that persons are not to be persecuted for cause of conscience.

Truth. And I believe (dear Peace) it shall appear to them that (with fear and trembling at the Word of the Lord) examine these passages, that the charge of error reboundeth back, even such an error as may well be called the bloody tenent, so directly contradicting the spirit and mind and practice of the Prince of peace, so deeply guilty of the blood of souls compelled and forced to hypocrisy in a spiritual and soul rape, so deeply guilty of the blood of the souls under the altar, persecuted in all ages for the cause of conscience, and so destructive to the civil peace and welfare of all kingdoms, countries, and commonwealths.

Peace. To this conclusion (dear Truth) I heartily subscribe, and know that God, the Spirit, the Prince, the angels and all true awakened sons of peace will call thee blessed.

Truth. How sweet and precious are these contemplations, but oh, how sweet the actions and fruitions?

Peace. Thy lips drop as the honeycomb, honey and milk are under thy tongue; oh that these drops, these streams might flow without a stop or interruption!

Truth. The glorious white troopers shall in time be mounted, and He that is the most high Prince of princes and the Lord General of generals, mounted upon the Word of truth and meekness, shall triumph gloriously and renew our meetings. But hark! what noise is this?

Peace. These are the doleful drums and shrill sounding trumpets, the roaring murdering cannons, the shouts of conquerors, the groans of wounded, dying, slaughtered—righteous with the wicked. Dear Truth, how long? How long these dreadful sounds and direful sights? How long before my glad return and restitution?

Truth. Sweet Peace, who will believe my true report? Yet true it is, if I were once believed, blest Truth and Peace should not so soon be parted.

Peace. Dear Truth, what welcome hast thou found of late beyond thy former times or present expectations?

Truth. Alas! my welcome changes as the times, and strongest swords and arms prevail. Were I believed in this, that Christ is not delighted with the blood of men (but shed His own for His bloodiest enemies), that by the Word of Christ no man for gainsaying Christ or joining with His enemy Antichrist should be molested with the civil sword—were this foundation laid as the Magna Charta of the highest liberties, and good security given on all hands for the preservation of it, how soon would every brow and house be stuck with olive branches?

[Having disposed, sentence by sentence, of Cotton's "Answer," Williams turns Peace and Truth to an equally detailed refutation of *A Model of Church and Civil Power.*]

Truth. I observe upon the point of delinquency such a confusion as heaven and earth may stand amazed at: "If the church offend," say they, "after advice refused, in conclusion the magistrate must redress, that is, punish the church (that is, in church offenses and cases) by a course of civil justice. On the other side, if the civil magistrate offend after admonition used, and not prevailing, in conclusion the church proceeds to censure, that is, to excommunication."

Now I demand, if the church be a delinquent, who shall judge? It is answered, the magistrate. Again, if the magistrate be a delinquent, I ask who shall judge? It is answered, the church. Whence I observe (which is monstrous in all cases in the world) that one person, to wit, the church or magistrate, shall be at one time the delinquent at the bar and the judge upon the bench. This is clear thus: the church must judge when the magistrate offends; and yet the magistrate must judge when the church offends, and so consequently in this case must judge whether she contemn civil authority in the Second Table for thus dealing with him, or whether she have broken the rules of the First Table, of which (say they) God hath made him keeper and conserver. And therefore, though the church make him a delinquent at the bar, yet by their confession God hath made him a judge on the bench. What blood, what tumults, hath been and must be spilt upon these grounds?

Truth. Here are divers particulars affirmed marvelous destructive both to godliness and honesty, though under a fair mask and color of both:

First, it will appear that in spiritual things they make the garden and the wilderness (as often I have intimated)—I say, the garden and the wilderness, the church and the world are all one. For thus:

If the powers of the world or civil state are bound to propose external peace in all godliness for their end, and the end of the church be to preserve internal peace in all godliness—I demand, if their end (godliness) be the same, is not their power and state the same also? Unless they make the church subordinate to the commonwealth's end, or the commonweal subordinate to the church's end, which (being the governor and setter-up of it, and so consequently the judges of it), it cannot be.

Now if godliness be the worshipping and walking with God in Christ, is not the magistrate and commonweal charged more by this tenent with the worship and ordinances of God than the church? For the magistrate they charge with the external peace in godliness, and the church but with the internal.

I ask further, what is this internal peace in all godliness? Whether intend they internal within the soul, which only the eye of God can see, opposed to external and visible, which man also can discern? Or else, whether they mean internal, that is, spiritual soul matters, matters of God's worship? And then I say that peace (to wit, of godliness or God's worship) they had before granted to the civil state.

Peace. The truth is (as I now perceive) the best and most godly of that judgment declare themselves never to have seen a true difference between the church and the world, and the spiritual and civil state. And howsoever these worthy Authors seem to make a kind of separation from the world, and profess that the church must consist of spiritual and living stones, saints, regenerate persons— and so make some peculiar enclosed ordinances, as the Supper of the Lord, which none, say they, but godly persons must taste of—yet by compelling all within their jurisdiction to an outward conformity of the church worship, of the Word and prayer, and maintenance of the ministry thereof, they evidently declare that they still lodge and dwell in the confused mixtures of the unclean and clean, of the flock of Christ and herds of the world together, I mean in spiritual and religious worship.

Truth. Whereas they say that the civil power may erect and establish what form of civil government may seem in wisdom most meet, I acknowledge the proposition to be most true, both in itself and also considered with the end of it, that a civil government is an ordinance of God to conserve the civil peace of people so far as concerns their bodies and goods.

But for this grant, I infer that the sovereign, original, and foundation of civil power lies in the people (whom thy must needs mean by the civil power distinct from the government set up). And if so, that a people may erect and establish what form of government seems to them most meet for their civil condition. It is evident that such governments as are by them erected and established have no more power, nor for no longer time, than the civil power or people consenting and agreeing shall betrust them with. This is clear not only in reason but in the experience of all commonweals where the people are not deprived of their natural freedom by the power of tyrants.

And if so—that the magistrates receive their power of governing the church from the people—undeniably it follows that a people, as a people, naturally considered (of what nature or nation soever, in Europe, Asia, Africa, or America) have fundamentally and originally, as men, a power to govern the church, to see her do her duty, to correct her, to redress, reform, establish, &c. And if this be not to pull God and Christ and Spirit out of heaven, and subject them unto natural, sinful, inconstant men—and so consequently to Satan himself, by whom all peoples naturally are guided—let heaven and earth judge.

Peace. It cannot by their own grant be denied but that the wildest Indians in America ought (and in their kind and several degrees do) to agree upon some forms of government: some more civil, compact in towns, and some less. And also that their civil and earthly governments be as lawful and true as any governments in the world, and therefore consequently their governors are keepers of the church or both Tables (if any church of Christ should arise or be amongst them): and therefore lastly (if Christ have betrusted and charged the civil power with His church), they must judge according to their Indian or American consciences, for other consciences it cannot be supposed they should have.

Peace. Again (say they) the magistrate should send him [a heretic] first to the church to heal his conscience [before taking civil action]. . . .

Truth. If a man thus bound be sent to a church to be healed in his conscience, either he is an heretic or he is not.

Admit he be: yet he disputes in fear, as the poor thief, the mouse, disputes with a terrible persecuting cat, who while she seems to play and gently toss, yet the conclusion is a proud, insulting, and devouring cruelty.

If no heretic but an innocent and faithful witness of any truth of Jesus: disputes he not as a lamb in the lion's paw, being sure in the end to be torn in pieces?

Peace. They add, "The censure this way proceeds with more power and blessing."

Truth. All power and blessing is from that blessed Son of God, unto whom all power is given from the Father, in heaven and earth. He hath promised His presence with His messengers, preaching and baptizing to the world's end, ratifying in heaven what they bind or loose on earth.

But let any man show me such a commission, instruction, and promise given by the Son of God to civil powers in these spiritual affairs of His Christian kingdom and worship.

Peace. Lastly they conclude, "This course of first sending the heretic to be healed by the church takes away all excuse: for none can say that he is persecuted for his conscience, but for sinning against his conscience."

Truth. Jezebel's placing poor Naboth before the elders as a blasphemer of God and the king, and sanctifying the plotted and intended murder with a day of humiliation, may seem to take away all excuse and to conclude the blasphemer worthy to be stoned. But Jehovah, the God of recompences, when He makes inquisition for blood, will find both Jezebel and Ahab guilty, and make the dogs a feast with the flesh of Jezebel, and leave not to Ahab a man to piss against the wall. For (as Paul in his own plea) there was nothing committed worthy of death: "And against thee, O King," saith Daniel, "I have not sinned in any civil fact against the state."

[The "typological" doctrine of church and state.]

Peace. Oh, that my head were a fountain and mine eyes rivers of tears, to lament my children, the children of

peace and light, thus darkening that and other lightsome
Scriptures with such dark and direful clouds of blood!

Truth. Sweet Peace, thy tears are seasonable and precious, and bottled up in the heavens; but let me add a
second consideration from that Scripture: if that Scripture
may now literally be applied to nations and cities in a
parallel to Canaan and Jerusalem since the Gospel, and
this Psalms 101 be literally to be applied to cities, towns,
and countries in Europe and America—not only such as
essay to join themselves (as they here speak) in a corrupt
church estate, but such as know no church estate, nor God,
nor Christ, yea, every wicked person and evil doer, must
be hanged or stoned, as it was in Israel. And if so, how
many thousands and millions of men and women in the
several kingdoms and governments of the world must be
cut off from their lands and destroyed from their cities? . . .

God gave unto that national church of the Jews that
excellent land of Canaan, and therein houses furnished,
orchards, gardens, vineyards, olive fields, wells, &c. They
might well in this settled abundance and promised continuation of it afford a large temporal supply to their
priests and levites, even to the tenth of all they did possess.

God's people are now in the Gospel brought into a spiritual land of Canaan, flowing with spiritual milk and
honey, and they abound with spiritual and heavenly com-
forts, though in a poor and persecuted condition: therefore, an enforced settled maintenance is not suitable to the
Gospel as it was to the ministry of priests and levites in
the law. . . .

The Lord expressly calls it His own land. . . . But now
the partition wall is broken down, and in respect of the
Lord's special propriety to one country more than another,

what difference between Asia and Africa, between Europe and America, between England and Turkey, London and Constantinople? . . .

What land, what country now is Israel's parallel and antitype but that holy mystical nation, the church of God, peculiar and called out to Him out of every nation and country? In which every true spiritual Naboth hath his spiritual inheritance, which he dare not part with though it be to his king or sovereign, and though such his refusal cost him this present life.

The people of Israel were all the seed or offspring of one man, Abraham. . . . But now, few nations of the world but are a mixed seed, the people of England especially: the Britons, Picts, Romans, Saxons, Danes, and Normans, by a wonderful providence of God being become one English people.

Only the spiritual Israel and seed of God, the newborn, are but one: Christ is the seed, and they only that are Christ's are only Abraham's seed and heirs. . . . This spiritual seed is the only antitype of the former figurative and typical: a seed which all Christians ought to propagate, yea even the unmarried men and women (who are not capable of natural offspring), for thus is this called the seed of Christ (who lived and died unmarried).

'Tis true, the people of Israel, brought into covenant with God in Abraham and so successively born in covenant with God, might (in that state of a national church) sol-

emnly covenant and swear that whosoever would not seek
Jehovah, the God of Israel, should be put to death, whether
small or great, whether man or woman.

But may whole nations or kingdoms now (according to
any one title expressed by Christ Jesus to that purpose)
follow that pattern of Israel and put to death all, both men
and women, great and small, that according to the rules of
the Gospel are not born again, penitent, humble, heavenly
patient? What a world of hypocrisy from hence is practiced by thousands that for fear will stoop to give that God
their bodies in a form whom yet in truth their hearts affect
not?

Yea, also, what a world of profanation of the holy name
and holy ordinances of the Lord in prostituting the holy
things of God to profane, impenitent, and unregenerate
persons?

What slaughters both of men and women must this
necessarily bring into the world, by insurrections and civil
wars about religion and conscience? Yea, what slaughters
of the innocent and faithful witnesses of Christ Jesus, who
choose to be slain all the day long for Christ His sake, and
to fight for the Lord and Master, Christ, only with spiritual
and Christian weapons?

Peace. Dear Truth, thou conquerest and shall triumph
in season: but some will say, "How answer you those
Scriptures alleged?"

Truth. I have fully and at large declared the vast differences between that holy nation of typical Israel and all
other lands and countries: how unmatchable then and

now, and never to be paralleled but by the true Israel and particular churches of Christ residing in all parts (and under the several civil governments) of the world. In which churches, the Israel of God and kingdom of Christ Jesus, such only are to be chosen spiritual officers and governors, to manage His kingly power and authority in the church, as are (according to the Scriptures quoted, not pope, bishops or civil powers, but) from amongst themselves, brethren fearing God, hating covetousness or filthy lucre, according to those golden rules given by the Lord Jesus.

The want of discerning this true parallel between Israel in type then and Israel the antitype now is that rock whereon (through the Lord's righteous jealousy, punishing the world and chastising His people) thousands dash and make woeful shipwreck.

The second branch, *viz.*, that all freemen elected be only church members,[15] I have before shown to be built on that sandy and dangerous ground of Israel's pattern. O, that it may please the Father of lights to discover this to all that fear His name! Then would they not sin to save a kingdom; nor run into the lamentable breach of civil peace and order in the world; nor be guilty of forcing thousands to hypocrisy in a state worship, nor of profaning the holy name of God and Christ by putting their names and ordinances upon unclean and unholy persons; nor of shedding the blood of such heretics whom Christ would have enjoy longer patience and permission until the harvest; nor of the blood of the Lord Jesus Himself, in His faithful witnesses of truth; nor lastly, of the blood of so many hundred thousands slaughtered men, women, and children, by such uncivil and unchristian wars and combustions about the Christian faith and religion.

Those former types of the land, of the people, of their worships, were types and figures of spiritual land, spiritual people, and spiritual worship under Christ. Therefore, consequently their saviors, redeemers, deliverers, judges, kings must also have their spiritual antitypes, and so consequently not civil but spiritual governors and rulers—lest the very essential nature of types, figures and shadows be overthrown. . . .

And yet the Israel of God now, the regenerate or newborn, the circumcised in heart by repentance and mortification, who willingly submit unto the Lord Jesus as their only king and head, may fitly parallel and answer that Israel in the type without such danger of hypocrisy, of such horrible profanations, and of firing the civil state in such bloody combustions as all age have brought forth upon this compelling a whole nation or kingdom to be the antitype of Israel.

Peace. Were this light entertained, some hopes would shine forth for my return and restoration.

[The conclusion.]

Peace. We have now (dear Truth) through the gracious hand of God clambered up to the top of this our tedious discourse.

Truth. O, 'tis mercy unexpressible that either thou or I have had so long a breathing time, and that together!

Peace. If English ground must yet be drunk with English blood, O, where shall Peace repose her wearied head and heavy heart?

Truth. Dear Peace, if thou find welcome, and the God of peace miraculously please to quench these all-devouring flames, yet where shall Truth find rest from cruel persecutions?

Peace. Oh, will not the authority of Holy Scriptures, the commands and declarations of the Son of God therein produced by thee, together with all the lamentable experiences of former and present slaughters, prevail with the sons of men (especially with the sons of peace) to depart from the dens of lions and mountains of leopards, and to put on the bowels (if not of Christianity, yet) of humanity, each to other!

Truth. Dear Peace, Habakkuk's fish keep their constant bloody game of persecution in the world's mighty ocean, the greater taking, plundering, swallowing up the lesser. O, happy he whose portion is the God of Jacob! who hath nothing to lose under the sun, but hath a state, a house, an inheritance, a name, a crown, a life, past all the plunderers', ravishers', murderers' reach and fury!

Peace. But lo! Who's here?

Truth. Our sister Patience, whose desired company is as needful as delightful. 'Tis like the wolf will send the scattered sheep in one; the common pirate gather up the loose and scattered navy; the slaughter of the witnesses by that bloody beast unite the Independents and Presbyterians. The God of Peace, the God of Truth, will shortly seal this truth and confirm this witness, and make it evident to the whole world:

That the doctrine of persecution for cause of conscience

is most evidently and lamentably contrary to the doctrine
of Christ Jesus, the Prince of peace. Amen.

IV

Returning in triumph to Providence in September 1644
(a flotilla of fourteen canoes met him and escorted him to
the dock), Williams plunged himself into a complex struggle not only with his still grasping neighbors, the colonies
of Massachusetts and Connecticut—barely held in check
by the charter—but also with the ferocious internal parties
of the small colony itself. Foremost among the groups now
making up the crazy quilt of Rhode Island were the Baptists—or, as they were then called, the Anabaptists.

Back in March of 1639 Williams was moved by the appeal of the first Baptist arrivals, and had supposed mo-
mentarily that in their principles of adult conversion and
renunciation of infant baptism might consist the pure
church emancipated from Judaic precedent. So he let himself be baptized by Ezekial Holliman, and for a few weeks
thereafter baptized others, but by the middle of the summer he decided—as he was always bound to decide—that
even a society so freely formed was still too sacerdotal.
He told the younger Winthrop in 1649 that the Baptist way
came nearer the first manner of Christianity than any
other, "and yet I have satisfaction neither in the authority
by which it is done, nor in the manner; nor in the prophecies concerning the rising of Christ's kingdom after the
desolation by Rome." Wrapped in these speculations,
while his great enemy in the colony, William Coddington,
called him "a mere weathercock, constant only in his un-

constancy," Williams became a "Seeker," forever looking for, hoping for, and on this earth never expecting to find an incorporated fellowship of Christ.

But the Baptists remained his friends, and their leader, John Clarke, of Newport, was his chief support. In July 1651 Clarke and his colleague Obadiah Holmes secretly penetrated to Lynn in Massachusetts to comfort a dying Anabaptist who somehow had stayed on there. John Winthrop was dead since 1649, and the governor was Williams' former friend and his betrayer at Salem, John Endecott. Clarke and Holmes were arrested, forced to listen to a sermon by John Cotton justifying the severest inflictions, were struck in the face by John Wilson, and cursed by both him and Endecott; they were fined and sentenced to be whipped. Friends paid Clarke's fine, but Holmes was lashed thirty times with a three-pronged whip.

Meanwhile, English Independents had followed the course Williams had predicted, and though some of them were reluctant, most of them, especially their champion Cromwell, became advocates of freedom of conscience— or at least freedom for all varieties of Puritans. When Clarke and Holmes found their way back to Rhode Island, Williams sent off, in the white heat of fury, this letter to Endecott, to which that one-time friend replied that he would try to give "satisfaction as much as lies in me." But Williams knew where the letter would have most effect; he kept a copy and carried it the next year to London, where by publishing it as an appendix to his book he helped materially to widen the breach between the Independents and their former brethren, and thus to further that isolation of orthodox New England which, as Williams saw it, was clearly a divine retribution upon persecutors.

The Copie of a Letter of R. Williams of Provi-
dence in New England, to Major Endicot, Gov-
ernour of the Massachusetts, upon occasion of the
late persecution against Mr. Clarke and Obadiah
Holmes, and others at Boston the chiefe Towne
of the Massachusetts in New England

Providence, August, 1651

Sir:

HAVING done with our transitory, earthly affairs,[16] which
in comparison of heavenly and eternal you will say are but
as dung and dross, let me now be humbly bold to remember that humanity and piety which I and others have
formerly observed in you, and in that hopeful remembrance to crave your gentle audience with patience and
mildness, with ingenuity, equanimity, and candor to him
that ever truly and deeply loved you and yours, and as in
the awful presence of His holy eye, whose dreadful hand
hath formed us to the praise of His mercy or justice to all
eternity. . . .

I have to say elsewhere about the causes of my banishment. . . . At present, let it not be offensive in your eyes
that I single out another, a fourth point, a cause of my
banishment also, wherein I greatly fear one or two sad
evils which hath befallen your soul and conscience.

The point is that of the civil magistrate's dealing in matters of conscience and religion, as also of persecuting and
hunting any for any matter merely spiritual and religious.

The two evils intimated are these: First, I fear you can
not after so much light and so much profession to the contrary (not only to myself, and so often in private, but)

before so many witnesses—I say, I fear you can not say and act so much, against so many several consciences, former and later, but with great checks, great threatenings, great blows and throes of inward conscience.

Secondly, if you shall thank God that it is not so with you, but that you do what conscience bids you in God's presence, upon God's warrant, I must then be humbly faithful to tell you that I fear your underprizing of holy light hath put out the candle and the eye of conscience in these particulars, and that delusions, strong delusions, and that from God (by Satan's subtleties), hath seized upon your very soul's belief, because you prized not, loved not, the endangered, persecuted Son of God in His despised truths and servants. . . .

Be pleased then (honored Sir) to remember that that thing which we call conscience is of such a nature (especially in Englishmen) as once a Pope of Rome, at the suffering of an Englishman in Rome, himself observed that although it be groundless, false, and deluded, yet it is not by any arguments or torments easily removed.

I speak not of the stream of the multitude of all nations, which have their ebbings and flowings in religion (as the longest sword and strongest arm of flesh carries it), but I speak of conscience, a persuasion fixed in the mind and heart of man, which enforceth him to judge (as Paul said of himself a persecutor) and to do so and so with respect to God, His worship.

This conscience is found in all mankind, more or less: in Jews, Turks, Papists, Protestants, pagans. And to this purpose let me freely without offense remember you (as I did Mr. Clarke newly come up from his sufferings amongst you)—I say, remember you of the same story I did him:

'twas that of William Hartley,[17] in Queen Elizabeth her days, who receiving the sentence of hanging and drawing, spake confidently (as afterwards he suffered), "What tell you me of hanging? If I had ten thousand millions of lives, I would spend them all for the Faith of Rome." . . .

I confess, that for confidence no Romish priest hath ever exceeded the martyrs or witnesses of Jesus: witness (amongst so many) that holy English woman who cried out that if every hair of her head were a life or man, they should burn for the name of the Lord Jesus. But Sir, your principles and conscience bind you not to respect Romish or English, saints or sinners: William Hartley and that woman, with all their lives, you are bound by your conscience to punish and (it may be) to hang or burn if they transgress against your conscience; and that because, according to Mr. Cotton's monstrous distinction (as some of his chief brethren to my knowledge hath called it), not because they sin in matters of conscience (which he denies the magistrate to deal in), but because they sin against their conscience. . . .

We not only use to say proverbially, but the Spirit of God expressly tells us, that there is a mind-bewitching, a bewitching of the very consciences and spirits of men. As in witchcraft, a stronger and supernatural power lays hold upon the powers of nature, with a suppressing or elevating of those powers beneath or above themselves: so it is with the very spirits and consciences of the most intelligent and conscientious when the Father of spirits is pleased in his righteous displeasure and jealousy so to suffer it to be with ours.

Sir, I from my soul honor and love the persons of such whom I, you, and themselves may see have been instrumental in your bewitching. Why should it be thought inconsistent with the holy wisdom of God to permit wise and holy and learned persons to wander themselves and mislead others when the holy Scripture and experience tell us of the dangerous counsels and ways of as wise and learned and holy as now breath in either old or New England air? . . .

The Maker and Searcher of our hearts knows with what bitterness I write, as with bitterness of soul I have heard such language as to proceed from yourself and others, who formerly have fled from (with crying out against) persecutors: "You will say, this is your conscience; you will say, you are persecuted, and you are persecuted for your conscience. No, you are conventiclers, heretics, blasphemers, seducers. You deserve to be hanged; rather than one shall be wanting to hang him, I will hang him myself. I am resolved not to leave an heretic in the country. I had rather so many whores and whoremongers and thieves came amongst us."

Oh Sir, you cannot forget what language and dialect this is, whether not the same unsavory and ungodly, blasphemous and bloody, which the Gardiners and Bonners, both former and latter, used to all that bowed not the state golden image of what conscience soever they were. And indeed, Sir, if the most High be pleased to awaken you to render unto His holy Majesty His due praises, in your truly broken-hearted confessions and supplications, you will then proclaim to all the world, that what profession soever you made of the Lamb, yet these expressions could not proceed from the dragon's mouth.

Oh remember, and the most holy Lord bring it to your remembrance, that you have now a great price in your

hand, to bring great glory to His holy name, great rejoicing
to so gracious a Redeemer (in whom you profess is all
your healing and salvation), great rejoicing to the holy
spirit of all true consolation whom yet so long you have
grieved and sadded, great rejoicing to those blessed spirits
(attending upon the Lamb and all His, and terrible to His
persecutors)—great rejoicing and instruction to all that
love the true Lord Jesus (notwithstanding their wander-
ings among so many false Christs), mourning and lament-
ing after Him in all parts of the world where His name is
sounded. Your talents are great, your fall hath been so:
your eminence is great, the glory of the most high in mercy
and justice toward you will be great also.

Oh, remember it is a dangerous combat for the potsherds
of the earth to fight with their dreadful potter! It is a dis-
mal battle for poor naked feet to kick against the pricks;
it is a dreadful voice from the King of kings and Lord of
lords: "Endecott, Endecott, why huntest thou me? why
imprisonest thou me? why finest, why so bloodily whip-
pest? why wouldst thou (did not I hold thy bloody hands)
hang and burn me?" Yea, Sir, I beseech you remember
that it is a dangerous thing to put this to the may-be, to the
venture or hazard, to the possibility. "Is it possible," may
you well say, "that since I hunt, I hunt not the life of my
Savior and the blood of the Lamb of God? I have fought
against many several sorts of consciences; is it beyond all
possibility and hazard that I have not fought against God,
that I have not persecuted Jesus in some of them?"

Sir, I must be humbly bold to say that 'tis impossible for
any man or men to maintain their Christ by their sword
and to worship a true Christ, to fight against all consciences
opposite to theirs, and not to fight against God in some of

them and to hunt after the precious life of the true Lord Jesus Christ. Oh, remember, whither your principles and consciences must in time and opportunity force you! 'Tis but worldly policy and compliance with men and times (God's mercy overruling) that holds your hands from the murdering of thousands and ten thousands, were your power and command as great as once the bloody Roman emperor's was. . . .

But oh, poor dust and ashes, like stones once rolling down the Alps, like the Indian canoes or English boats loose and adrift, where stop we until infinite mercy stop us, especially when a false fire of zeal and confidence drives us, though against the most holy and eternal Himself? . . .

'Twas mercy infinite that stopped provoked justice from blowing out our candles in our youths; but now the feeding substance of the candles is gone, and 'tis impossible (without repentance) to recall our actions! Nay, with repentance, to recall our minutes past us.

Sir, I know I have much presumed upon your many weighty affairs and thoughts; I end with an humble cry to the Father of mercies, that you may take David's counsel, and silently commune with your own heart upon your bed, reflect upon your own spirit, and believe Him that said it to his over-zealous disciples, "You know not what spirit you are of"; that no sleep may seize upon your eyes, nor slumber upon your eyelids, until your serious thoughts have seriously, calmly, and unchangeably (through help from Christ Jesus) fixed,

First, on a moderation towards the spirits and consciences of all mankind, merely differing from or opposing yours with only religious and spiritual opposition;

Secondly, a deep and cordial resolution (in these wonderful searching, disputing, and dissenting times) to search, to listen, to pray, to fast, and more fearfully, more tremblingly to enquire what the holy pleasure and the holy mysteries of the most Holy are: in whom I humbly desire to be

> Your poor fellow-servant, unfeignedly,
> respective and faithful,
> *Roger Williams*

V

John Cotton had no choice, once copies of Williams' publications of 1644 were rushed from the boat to his study, but to settle down to rebuttal. He betrays that he was tired, and more than a little frightened, because every dispatch told of the perfidy of the Independents and the decline of his and New England's prestige among Cromwell's troopers. But for the honor of Massachusetts as well as for his own he had to take up the challenge, and in 1647 his two dutiful answers were published in London.

A Reply to Mr. Williams his Examination goes painfully over the history of Williams' banishment, less occupied with justifying the sentence than with exonerating Cotton. Because Williams had paraded Cotton's near escape from disaster in the Hutchinson affair of 1637, Cotton had to tell his part in that crisis also, thus composing several of the most labored and evasive pages ever written by a Puritan. The *Reply* makes abundantly clear how much Cotton hated Williams. Where Williams had said that many in Massachusetts held him truly godly, Cotton sneers, "I did never perceive just ground for such public acknowledgment." He declares that Williams from the beginning was "self-pleasing, self-full, or (as it is translated) self-willed," that he was nothing but "a haberdasher of small questions."

But *The Bloudy Tenent* was a more serious matter; Cotton went through it chapter by chapter, ringing changes on his great distinction—the one Williams told Endecott was monstrous—between unjust persecution for conscience and legitimate punishment of a conscience that sinned against itself. The result was *The Bloudy Tenent, Washed, And made white in the bloud of the Lambe: Being Discussed and Discharged of Bloud-guiltinesse by just Defence.* It and the *Reply* were separately paged but bound in a single cover, and copies were promptly shipped to Providence.

Internal evidence indicates that Williams composed his answer in Rhode Island and sent the manuscript to London before he and John Clarke sailed from Boston (November 1651) in order to protect the charter against the ravages of their domestic enemy, Coddington. In June 1650 Williams reminded the younger Winthrop that in dealing with the *Model* in *The Bloudy Tenent* he had "been large in the difference between that land of Israel and all others," but that Cotton, on the plea that he was not an author of the *Model*, sidestepped this fundamental issue. Williams begged Winthrop to tell him whether there was any discussion of it in orthodox New England, for "'tis a controversy wherein I am deeply engaged, of which you will (if God please) see more." Even so, Clarke published ahead of him, on May 13, 1652, *Ill Newes from New-England: or a Narrative of New-Englands Persecution,* informing an England whose rulers were now shocked

by such proceedings what sufferings he, Holmes, and the
Baptists had endured in America. Williams made hasty
additions to his manuscript in order to include the Baptists'
story, appended his letter to Endecott, and at the end of
May, or possibly in June 1652, brought out *The Bloody
Tenent yet More Bloody: By Mr. Cottons endevour to
wash it white in the Blood of the Lambe.*

The modern mind finds this succession of "bloudy tenents," with their lengthening titles, infinitely comic (Cotton would surely have had to come back with a still longer
one had he not died in 1652, probably before he saw Williams' book), but an age that reveled in technical disputation relished the spectacle. *The Bloody Tenent yet More
Bloody* goes over the same ground as *The Bloudy Tenent,*
adding no new ideas or arguments, but much rhetoric. It
makes confusing reading, for there are now five instead
of merely three strata: the Anabaptist "Author"; John Cotton as "Answerer"; Williams (in *The Bloudy Tenent*) as
"Discusser"; John Cotton (in *The Bloudy Tenent,
Washed*) as the "Defender"; and finally Williams, once
more speaking through Peace and Truth. This formidable
structure frightens away all but the most patient student,
and the book has been honored more by citation of the
title than by actual perusal. Although Peace generally
quotes enough of Cotton to provide Truth with a target,
Williams assumes that the reader has *The Bloudy Tenent,
Washed* in mind or actually beside him. It would be
tedious, even were there space, to reproduce much of this
pyramided discussion. In order to make the debate as
clear as possible, on four major points I have inter-
posed, in brackets, Cotton's statements from *The Bloudy
Tenent, Washed,* taking the liberty to explain the problem

in order that the effectiveness of Williams' hard-hitting
replies may be brought out.

Williams now, as compared with 1644, was riding high,
for he had such friends as Milton and Vane to encourage
him, and Cromwell more or less on his side. Cotton complained that Williams, in publishing both the *Letter* and
the "Answer," violated all rules of decency, since these
were private papers. Williams taunted him back: "What
breach of rule can Master Cotton say it was to answer that
in the streets which Master Cotton proclaimeth on the
housetops?" He took a wicked delight in noting that while
Cotton essayed to deal with *The Bloudy Tenent* piece-by-
piece, he ignored the prefatory address to Parliament; Williams was exacting a pound of flesh for all he had suffered
in 1635 and 1636 by explaining in 1652 why Cotton seemed
so blind:

I desire my rejoinder may be as full of love as truth; yet
some say Master Cotton is wise and knows in what door
the wind blows of late; he is not ignorant what sad complaints in letters, printing, conferences, so many of God's
people (and of his own conscience and judgment of Independency) have poured forth against New England's persecuting. He knows what bars New England's bloody tenent and practice may put to his brethren's just desires and
suits for moderation and toleration to non-conforming
consciences.

Cotton is compelled to write, forced by his own conscience "and the credit of his way," but nowadays "the
times advise him" to attract as little attention to himself as
possible lest "that high and searching house of England's
Parliament should search and scan his meditations."

Therefore, in order to direct as much as possible of this

unwanted attention on Cotton and Massachusetts, Williams opened with two prefaces: the first, an address to Parliament, could now become a hymn of praise; the second—the real preface—was an address to the General Courts of orthodox and respectable New England. Perhaps the most prophetic element in the whole debate is that both in 1644 and 1652 Williams had to go to London, and there, by arousing a European awareness, fight America's battle.

The Bloody Tenent yet More Bloody: by Mr. Cottons endevour to wash it white in the Blood of the Lambe
By R. Williams of Providence in New-England
London, 1652

To the several respective General Courts, especially that of Massachusetts in New England

Honored and beloved Friends and Countrymen:
WHILE you sit dry on your safe American shores (by God's most gracious providence) and have beheld the doleful tossings of so many of Europe's nations, yea, of our dearest mother, aged England, in a sea of tears and blood, I am humbly bold to present your eyes and hearts with this (not unseasonable) discourse of blood, of the bloody tenents of persecution, oppression, and violence, in the cause and matters of conscience and religion.

It is a second conference of Peace and Truth, an examination of the worthily honored and beloved Mr. Cotton's reply to a former conference and treatise of this subject. And although it concern all nations which have persecuted

and shed the blood of Jesus—the bloody Roman Empire
with all the savage lions thereof, emperors and popes, the
bloody monarchies of Spain and France, and the rest of
Europe's kingdoms and states (which under their several
vizards and pretenses of service to God have, in so many
thousands of His servants, murdered so many thousand
times over His dear Son), yea, although it concern that
bloody Turkish monarchy, and all the nations of the world
who practice violence to the conscience of any Christian, or
Antichristians, Jews or pagans—yet it concerns yourselves
(with all due respect otherwise be it spoken) in some more
eminent degrees. Partly as so many of yours of chief note
(beside Mr. Cotton) are engaged in it; partly as New England (in respect of spiritual and civil state) professeth to
draw nearer to Christ Jesus than other states and churches;
and partly as New England is believed to hold and practice such a bloody doctrine, notwithstanding Mr. Cotton's
veils and pretenses of not persecuting men for conscience,
but punishing them only for sinning against conscience!
And of but so and so, not persecuting but punishing heretics, blasphemers, idolaters, seducers, &c. . . .

But yet your consciences (as all men's) must be satisfied: I have therefore in all these agitations humbly
presented (amongst others) two fundamental hints or
considerations:

First, that the people (the original of all free power and
government) are not invested with power from Christ
Jesus to rule his wife or church, to keep it pure, to punish
opposites by force of arms;

Secondly, that the pattern of the national church of
Israel was a none-such, unimitable by any civil state in all
or any of the nations of the world beside. . . .

I add, it is a glorious character of every true disciple or scholar of Christ Jesus to be never too old to learn.

It is the command of Christ Jesus to his scholars to try all things: and liberty of trying what a friend, yea, what an (esteemed) enemy presents hath ever (in point of Christianity) proved one especial means of attaining to the truth of Christ.

For I dare confidently appeal to the consciences of God's most knowing servants if that observation be not true: to wit, that it hath been the common way of the Father of lights to enclose the light of His holy truths in dark and obscure—yea, and ordinarily in forbidden—books, persons, and meetings by Satan styled conventicles.

New English voyages have taught most of our old English spirits how to put due prices upon the most common and ordinary undervalued mercies: how precious with some hath been a little water? how dainty with others a piece of bread? how welcome to some the poorest housing? Yea, the very land and earth after long and tedious passages?

There is one commodity for the sake of which most of God's children in New England have run their mighty hazards: a commodity marvelously scarce in former times (though in some late years by God's most gracious and mighty hand more plentiful) in our native country: it is a liberty of searching after God's most holy mind and pleasure. . . .

Among the crying sins of our own or other sinful nations, those two are ever among the loudest—to wit, invented devotions to the God of heaven; secondly, violence and oppression on the sons of men (especially if His sons) for dissenting. And against both these, and that the impartial and dreadful hand of the most holy and jealous God (a consuming fire) tear and burn not up at last the roots of these plantations, but graciously discovering the plants which are not His, He may graciously fructify and cause to flourish what His right hand will own: I say this is the humble and unfeigned desire and cry (at the throne of grace) of your so long despised outcast,

Roger Williams

To the merciful and compassionate reader:

. . . Touching Mr. Cotton, although I rejoice that since it pleased God to lay a command on my conscience to come in as His poor witness in this great cause—I say, I rejoice it hath pleased him to appoint so able, and excellent, and conscionable an instrument to bolt out the truth to the bran. So I can humbly say it in His holy presence, it is my constant heaviness and soul's grief as to differ from any fearing God: so much more ten thousand times from Mr. Cotton, whom I have ever desired, and still desire, highly to esteem, and dearly love to respect for so great a portion of mercy and grace vouchsafed unto him, and so many truths of Christ Jesus maintained by him. And therefore (notwithstanding that some, of no common judgment and respect to him, have said that he wrote his washing of the bloody tenent in blood against Christ Jesus and gall against me, yet) if upon so slippery and narrow a passage I have slipped (notwithstanding my constant resolution to the contrary) into any term or expression unbeseeming his person or the matter (the cause of the most high in hand considered), I humbly crave pardon of God and Mr. Cotton also. . . .

But concerning his work, the observant reader will soon discover that whatever Mr. Cotton's stand is, yet he most weakly provides himself of very strange reserves and retreats. . . . When it is urged that through this whole book he persecutes or hunts (by name) the idolater, the blasphemer, the heretic, the seducer, and that to death or banishment, . . . Mr. Cotton retreats into the land of Israel, and calls up Moses and his laws against idolaters, blasphemers, seducers, &c. When he is challenged . . . for producing the pattern of a national church, when he stands only for a Congregational—for producing that national church of Israel, so miraculous, so typical, as a copy or sampler for the nations and peoples of the world (who have no such miraculous and typical respect upon them)—Mr. Cotton retreats to "moral equity," that the seducer and he that kills a soul should die.

When it is urged that Christ Jesus, at His so long typedout coming, abolished those national shadows and erected His spiritual kingdom, . . . Mr. Cotton retreats and confesseth Christ's kingdom is spiritual, not national but Congregational, and that those Scriptures hold forth a spiritual cutting off; and he so produceth them to prove the heretic to be cut off, alleging that the question was put in general terms, that he knew not what persecution should be intended, and that an unjust excommunication is as sore a persecution as an unjust banishment. When he is urged with the nature of the consciences (even of all men to God or Gods in their worship), he professeth that he is wronged and that he doth not hold that any man should be persecuted for his conscience, but for sinning against his conscience.

When all the consciences in the world cry out against

him for setting up the civil power and officers, the courts
of civil justice, to judge of the conviction of men's souls and
consciences, Mr. Cotton retreats to his last refuge, and
saith that although this be the duty of all the magistrates
in the world, yet not any of them must meddle to punish
in religion until they be informed, which is (upon the
point) until he is sure they will draw their swords for his
conscience, church, against all others as heretical, blasphemous.

The monstrous partiality of such suspending, of hanging
up all the magistrates in the world (except a few of his own
persuasion), and that from so principal and main a part of
their office, and that so many thousands in the nations of
the world all the world over, and that constantly and per-
petually all their days! If it please the most jealous and
righteous God to hide it (I say, the monstrousness of such
a suspension) from Mr. Cotton's eyes, yet thousands and
ten thousands will behold and wonder at it. . . .

I confess in this plea for freedom to all consciences in
matters (merely) of worship, I have impartially pleaded
for the freedom of the consciences of the Papists themselves, the greatest enemies and persecutors (in Europe)
of the saints and truths of Jesus: yet I have pleaded for no
more than is their due and right, and (whatever else shall
be the consequent) it shall stand for a monument and
testimony against them, and be an aggravation of their
former, present, or future cruelties against Christ Jesus the
head, and all that uprightly love Him, His true disciples
and followers.

It is true, I have not satisfaction in the clear discovery
of those holy prophecies and periods set down and prefixed
by the Holy Spirit in Daniel, John, &c., concerning the

kingdom of Christ Jesus. Yet two things I profess in the holy presence of God, angels, and men:

First, my humble desires and resolution (the Lord assisting) to contend for the true and visible worship of the true and living God, according to the institution and appointment of the last will and testament of Christ Jesus;

Second, I believe and profess that such persons, such churches, are got nearest to Christ Jesus on whose forehead are written these blessed characters of the true Lord Jesus Christ:

First, content with a poor and low condition in worldly things;

Second, an holy cleansing from the filthiness of false worships and worldly conversations;

Third, an humble and constant endeavor to attain (in their simplicity and purity) to the ordinances and appointments of Christ Jesus;

Fourth, are so far from smiting, killing, and wounding the opposites of their profession and worship that they resolve themselves patiently to bear and carry the cross and gallows of their Lord and Master, and patiently to suffer with Him.

In the number of such His poor servants who as unfeignedly desire (notwithstanding my plea against persecutors and persecution)—I say as unfeignedly desire to suffer as cheerfully with Christ Jesus as gloriously to reign with Him—desires to be,

> Thine unfeigned, though unworthiest of
> all the followers of Jesus,
> *Roger Williams*

Peace. In his description of "arrogancy" and "impetuousness," Master Cotton tells us that he that refuseth to subject his spirit to the spirit of the prophets, that shall oppose such as dissent with clubs, swords, and censorious reproaches, or reject communion with the church, his practice tends to the disturbing of civil or church peace, or both.

Truth. It is a fallacious mingling of clubs, swords, reproaches, with refusing to submit to the spirit of prophecy in the prophets and rejecting of communion. For a man may, out of true and upright conscience to God (as Master Cotton will not deny), refuse to submit to a whole true church, having the truth of God on his side—and may withdraw from communion with a church obstinate in sin —and this without breach of civil peace; and therefore the mingling or confounding these spiritual resistances or disturbances with guns, swords, &c., is a mingling and confounding of heaven and earth together.

In that he saith, "These ways tend to the disturbance of either civil or church peace, or both," he speaks too like the doubtful oracles of Apollo, which will be true however the event fall out. But yet he toucheth not the truth of the question, which concerns civil peace only; against the disturbers of which I grant the civil powers to be armed with a civil sword not in vain, and concerning which divers cases were propounded of seeming "arrogance" and "impetuousness" in God's servants; and yet they fell not justly under any censure of breach of civil peace.

Peace. "'Tis true," saith Master Cotton, "because they were not ways of arrogance nor impetuousness."

Truth. But will Master Cotton give way that any conscience but his own may freely preach and dispute against the state religion, freely reprove the highest, in sharpest language, for matter of religion—refuse conformity to the common established religion and worship, disclaim sub-

jection to the civil powers in spiritual cases—preach against
the common policy and seeming wisdom of the state, even
to a seeming hazarding of all—and lastly occasion great
tumults and uproars (which were the six cases alleged)?
If Master Cotton granteth this freedom to other consciences beside his own, why preacheth he persecution
against such a liberty which other consciences beside his
own believe they justly challenge? If to no other conscience than his own, it is not his saying ten thousand times
that his conscience is true and others false, nor any other
distinction in the world, can clear him from most unrighte-
ous and unchristian partiality. . . .

Peace. "It is a falsehood," saith Master Cotton, "that I
call the slight listenings of God's people to the checks of
their consciences their sinning against their conscience:
for I speak not of the sinning of God's people against conscience, but of an heretic subverted; much less do I call
their slight listening to conscience an heretical sinning
against conscience; least of all do I say that for slight listening to the checks of conscience, he may lawfully be persecuted as for sinning against his conscience." And he adds
this gall to the former vinegar: "Thus men that have time
and leisure-at-will set up images of clouts, and then shoot
at them." . . .

Truth. Questionless, no child of God but in temptation
may sin heretically—that is, obstinately upon once or twice
admonition—against the checks and whisperings of his own
conscience, and against that evidence of light which (afterward) he wondereth how he could despise: and this rejecting or casting forth of the visible society of Christ Jesus

and His servants is not for destruction, but humiliation and salvation in the day of the Lord Jesus.

Peace. I judge that no son of peace, in a sober and peaceable mind, can judge, as Master Cotton here doth, this to be an image of clouts?

Truth. Nor can I learn that the Discusser so aboundeth in time and leisure as to make such images as Master Cotton insinuates. It is not unknown to many witnesses in Plymouth, Salem, and Providence that the Discusser's time hath not been spent (though as much as any other's whosoever) altogether in spiritual labors and public exercise of the Word, but day and night, at home and abroad, on the land and water, at the hoe, at the oar, for bread; yea, and I can tell that when these discussions were prepared for public in London, his time was eaten up in attendance upon the service of the Parliament and city for the supply of the poor of the city with wood (during the stop of coal from Newcastle and the mutinies of the poor for firing[18]). 'Tis true, he might have run the road of preferment as well in old as in New England, and have had the leisure and time of such who eat and drink with the drunken and smite with the fist of wickedness their fellow servants. But God is a most holy witness that these meditations were fitted for public view in change of rooms and corners—yea, sometimes (upon occasion of travel in the country concerning that business of fuel) in variety of strange houses, sometimes in the fields in the midst of travel, where he hath been forced to gather and scatter his loose thoughts and papers.

Peace. Well, notwithstanding Master Cotton's bitter censure, some persons of not contemptible note nor intelligence have by letters from England informed the Dis-

cusser that these "images of clouts" it hath pleased God to
make use of to stop no small leaks of persecution that
lately began to flow in upon dissenting consciences, and
(amongst others) to Master Cotton's own, and to the peace
and quietness of the Independents, which they have so
long and so wonderfully enjoyed.

Truth. I will end this chapter with that famous distinction of the Lord Jesus: digging, begging, stealing are the
three ways by which all that pretend to be Christ's
stewards are maintained. They that cannot dig can beg
the glittering preferments of this present evil world and the
wages of Balaam. They that cannot dig can steal, in the
ways of fraud, oppression, extortion. But by the mercy of
the most high, the Discusser hath been enabled to get his
bread by as hard digging as most diggers in New or old
England have been put to. And let all men judge whether
such as can beg or steal and cannot dig, or such as choose
neither to beg nor steal but dig, have most time and leisure
to make such "images of clouts." . . .

[Further exposition of the parable of the tares and the
wheat:

Cotton agrees that the "field" may be the "world," yet
insists that in this parable Christ does not mean the wide
world "but (by an usual trope) the church scattered
through the world."

"It is not the will of Christ that Antichrist and Antichristians and Antichristianity should be tolerated in the
world until the end of the world. For God will put it into
the hearts of faithful princes (as they have given their
kingdoms to the beast, so) in fullness of time to hate the

whore, to leave her desolate and naked, and to burn her flesh with fire."

To this Williams must answer not with demonstrable refutation but with that wonder concerning the mystery of life which is at once both the strength and the weakness of a typologist.]

Truth. It is true that the world lieth in wickedness and is full of fornicators, idolaters, and yet it was some thousands of years when the world was not full of Christians—that is, "anointed or holy fornicators," "holy idolaters." That is indeed and in truth Antichristian, and that alone is the point in question, about which this answer of Master Cotton hovers but comes not near it. This is indeed a most dreadful and wonderful point of the wisdom, justice, and patience of God: so to suffer so many millions of men and women to arrogate to themselves the name and profession of the most holy living God, and His holy Son Christ Jesus, to be called Christians, anointed or holy, and yet upon the point to hate the holiness, truth, and spirit of Christ Jesus.

Peace. This is doubtless to me (whate'er Master Cotton imagines) a wonderful mystery in all ages since these tares were first sown: to see, I say, so many millions of holy idolaters, holy murderers, holy whoremongers, holy thieves.

The blasphemy of this is so wonderful and dreadful that I cannot sufficiently wonder at him that wonders not how this comes to pass. . . .

Truth. It is not said that those princes that shall hate the whore shall be faithful princes; and since Master Cotton seems to hold that by way of ordinance (and so in obedience) the kings of the earth shall with the sword destroy

Antichrist, I desire his proof for any such prophecy. For:

1. It is not said that God will put it into their hearts to hate the whore. And we find that they shall hate the Lamb as well as hate the whore. . . .

2. Judgment may be executed upon the whore by way of mutual judgment each upon others, when in the midst of their spiritual whoredoms and drunkenness with the saints' blood they shall fall out with the whore (as useth to be in whoredom), and turn their whorish loves into outrageous fury. And the very description of their fury looks this way, for it is not the property of sober and faithful men (though repenting of their whoredom) to make a woman naked (though a whore) and to eat her flesh, as it is said those shall do.

[Although most clearly trying to avoid a head-on collision over typology, Cotton finds himself once or twice obliged to confront it; in such a passage as this he gives away, against his will and inclination, the nub of the controversy:

"It is true, Christ hath appointed spiritual means for the avoiding and preventing the infection of heresies; so hath He also for the preventing and avoiding all offenses in church members. But that hindereth not the lawful and necessary use of a civil sword for the punishment of some such offenses as are subject to church censure. If indeed the ordinances of Christ in the church do prevail to the avoiding and healing of heresies, there is no need of the civil sword for that end. But it often falleth out otherwise. As:

"1. That when the church hath cast out an heretic, yet he still remaineth obstinate and proceedeth to seduce and destroy the faith of some (it may be of many). . . . If the magistrate's sword do here rust in the scabbard, such leaven may leaven the whole mass of city or country. . . .

"2. It may be the heretic was never any member of the church, and then though the church may lay in some antidotes and purges to preserve or recover their members—yet how shall they succor such as are not subject to their censures? Or how shall they prevent the spreading of this noisome leprosy in private conventicles?

"It is evident the civil sword was appointed for a remedy in this case. . . . And therefore it cannot truly be said that the Lord Jesus never appointed the civil sword for a remedy in such a case. For He did expressly appoint it in the Old Testament, nor did He ever abrogate it in the New. The reason of the law (which is the life of the law) is of eternal force and equity in all ages. . . . This reason is of moral —that is, of universal and perpetual—equity to put to death any apostate, seducing idolater, or heretic who seeketh to thrust away the souls of God's people from the Lord their God."

Here, more than in any previous statement, Cotton made clear what he meant by subversive, and here, in the name of a universal and timeless morality, delivered his most pertinent challenge to the relativistic, humane, and disillusioned doctrine of typology.]

Peace. The entrance of this chapter (dear Truth) looks in mine eye like one of the bloody fathers of the inquisition, and breathes (like Paul in his mad zeal and frenzy) slaughters against the Son of God Himself, though under the name or brand of a "seducer," as all persecutors have ever done.

Truth. Thy tender brain and heart cannot let fly an arrow sharp enough to pierce the bowels of such a bloody tenent.

Peace. The flaming jealousy of that most holy and righteous judge, who is a consuming fire, will not ever hear such tenents and behold such practices in silence.

Truth. Sweet Peace, long and long may the almond tree flourish on Master Cotton's head in the arms of true Christianity and true Christian honor. And let New England's colonies flourish also (if Christ so please), until He come again the second time! But that He who is love itself would please to tell Master Cotton and the colonies—and the world —the untrueness, uncharitableness, unmercifulness, and unpeaceableness of such conclusions. For is not this the plain English and the bottom—to wit, if the spirit of Christ Jesus in any of His servants, sons or daughters, witnessing against the abominations or sticks of Antichrist, shall persuade one soul, man or woman, to fear God, to come out of Babel, to refuse to bow down to and to come out from communion with a state-golden-image, and not to touch what it is persuaded is an unclean thing:

That man or woman who was the Lamb's and the Spirit's instruments thus to enlighten and persuade one soul, he hath (saith this tenent), laid a leaven which corrupteth the state—that is, the land, town, city, kingdom, or empire of the world; that leaven shall bring the captivity, ruin, and destruction of the state! And therefore *Lex Talionis:* not only soul for soul in the next, but life for life also in this present world! . . .

Peace. But, saith Master Cotton, false prophets in the Old Testament were to die but for attempting; and the reason was not from any typical holiness of the land but from the dangerous wickedness of the attempting to thrust away a soul from God, which is a greater injury than to deprive a man of bodily life.

Truth. The reason to me appears plainly typical with respect to that holy nation and the seducers seeking to turn the soul away from the Lord their God, who had brought them forth from the land of Egypt, by such signs, miracles. Let Master Cotton now produce any such nation in the whole world whom God in the New Testament hath literally and miraculously brought forth of Egypt, or from one land into another, to the truth and purity of his worship—then far be it but I should acknowledge that the seducer is fit to be put to death.[19] But draw away the curtain of the shadow and let the substance appear: not a whole nation, city, but the Christian church brought by spiritual signs and wonders from the Egypt of this world in all nations of the world where the Gospel comes. Justly, therefore, he that seduceth a soul from his God in Christ, and so endangereth to leaven the only true Christian state or kingdom, the church of Christ, he ought to die (upon his obstinacy) without mercy, as well under Christ as under Moses. Yea, he is worthy of a sorer punishment (as saith the Spirit of God) who trampleth under feet the blood of Christ: such a deceiver or seducer (except he repent) is to be cut from the presence of the Lord and to lose an eternal life. He that is cut off from material Israel might yet repent and live eternally, but he that is cut off from the mystical Israel under the Gospel—that is, for obstinacy in sin (the proper heretic)—he is cut off to all eternity: which punishment, as it is infinitely transcendent and more dreadful in the nature and kind of it, so answereth it fully and infinitely that clause of Master Cotton—to wit, "to thrust a soul from God is a greater injury than to deprive a man of his bodily life." . . .

Peace. Methinks, this answer may also fully satisfy his second supposition, to wit, if that the heretic was never of the church?

Truth. Yea, what hath the church to do (that is, judicially) with him that is without? And what hath the civil state to judge him for, who in civil matters hath not transgressed? In vain therefore doth Master Cotton suggest a persecuting or hunting after the souls or lives of such as, being cast out of the church, keep private conventicles.

Peace. How grievous is this language of Master Cotton, as if he had been nourished in the chapels and cloisters of persecuting prelates and priests, the Scribes and Pharisees? As if he never had heard of Jesus Christ in truth and meekness! For surely (as the Discusser observed), Christ Jesus never appointed the civil sword an antidote or remedy in such a case, notwithstanding Master Cotton replies that the civil sword was appointed a remedy in this case by Moses—not Christ. . . .

But Master Cotton proceedeth, alleging that the minister of God must have in readiness to execute vengeance on him that doth evil. "And evil it is," saith he, "to thrust away God's people from him."

Truth. Every lawful magistrate, whether succeeding or elected, is not only the minister of God but the minister or servant of the people also (what people or nation soever they be, all the world over), and that minister or magistrate goes beyond his commission who intermeddles with that which cannot be given him in commission from the people, unless Master Cotton can prove that all the people and inhabitants of all nations in the world have spiritual power—Christ's power—naturally, fundamentally, and originally residing in them (as they are people and inhabitants of this world) to rule Christ's spouse, the church, and to give spiritual power to their officers to exercise their spiritual laws and commands. Otherwise it is but profaning the holy name of the most high. It is but flattering of magistrates, it is but the accursed trusting to an arm of flesh, to persuade the rulers of the earth that they are kings of the Israel or church of God, who were in their institutions and government immediately from God the rulers and governors of His holy church and people. . . .

Peace. If neither the nations of the world, as peoples and nations, have received this power originally and fundamentally, nor can they derive it ministerially to their civil officers (by what name or title, high or low, soever they be distinguished)—Oh, what presumption, what profaning of God's most holy name, what usurpation over the souls and consciences of men, though it come under the veil or vizard of saving the city or kingdom, yea, of saving of souls and honoring of God himself?

[Again, in his Chapter L, Cotton lets himself be lured into an aside on typology:

"Though the nations now have not that typical holiness which the nation of Israel had, yet all the churches of the saints have as much truth and reality of holiness as Israel had. And therefore what holy care of religion lay upon the kings of Israel in the Old Testament, the same lieth

now upon Christian kings in the New Testament, to protect the same in their churches."

Here again, in the name of universal law and a pattern
for imitation, was the argument for American exceptional-
ism—the special place in history of these communities
which professedly approached the model of Israel. Williams had by now, both in formal argument and in passing
comment, made the issue clear; now he could only ex-
claim.]

Truth. Oh, how near the precious jewels and bargains of
truth come sometimes God's saints and yet miss of the finding and going through with it! The churches of the New
Testament, Master Cotton grants, succeed the Church of
Israel: the kings and governors thereof of the churches of
Christ must succeed those kings. What king and governors
of Israel are now to be found in the Gospel but Christ Jesus
and His servants deputed in His absence, which are all of a
spiritual consideration? What is this to the nations, kings,
and governors of the world, where few kings, few nobles,
few wise, are called to profess Christ? Is not Christ Jesus
the only King of Israel, and are not all His holy ones made
kings and priests unto God? And unto His saints, and His
spiritual officers' administration in the midst of them, is His
kingdom's power committed in His absence. This spiritual
power, however the pope and prelates, kings and princes,
Parliaments and General Courts, and their respective officers of justice (to be honored and obeyed in civil things)—
I say, however they have challenged and assumed this
kingly power of the Son of God, yet the King of kings,
Christ Jesus, hath begun to discover, and will never leave
until He hath made it clear as the sun's beams that He is

robbed of His crown, and will shake and break all the
nations and powers of the world until His heavenly crown
be again restored.

[As a final illustration of how the debate was carried on
—which speaks volumes for the two points of view—we
may note Cotton's reply to Williams' accusation that the
clergy of New England made the magistrates "stairs and
stirrups" for themselves to mount into rich and honorable
saddles, by which, Williams says, he meant their great and
settled maintenance, such as Christ never allowed to even
His own Apostles.

The clergy of New England were not sumptuously provided, and in all honesty considered themselves poor scholars. The church of Boston did indeed vote that it would
rely only on voluntary contributions, but throughout
Massachusetts and Connecticut ecclesiastical rates were
levied by law and collected by the sheriffs. Cotton had already equivocated about this matter; but what is more
interesting is his utter inability to comprehend Williams'
charge that the orthodox clergy fought against liberty of
conscience because they had a vested interest in the regime
of intolerance:

"How this power ascribed to magistrates, not by me but
by the body, almost, of all faithful ministers, yea, by the
prophets and Apostles themselves, should make magistrates stairs and stirrups for ourselves to mount up so high,
let him that can discern it, make it appear. To allow them
power over ourselves in case of heretical delinquency is
not to make them stairs or stirrups of our advancement, but
swords and staves (if need be) for our punishment.

"Besides, I wonder what fancy came into the Discusser's mind to dream of rich and honorable seats and saddles of our magistrates? Whenas he need not be ignorant how far short they themselves fall of rich and honorable seats and saddles, which itself interpreteth great and settled maintenances.

"Lastly, I suppose he is not ignorant that myself, against whom he is pleased by name to write this invective, liveth not upon great and settled maintenance but according to that which he calleth the true pattern of the first messengers of the Lord Jesus."]

Truth. It is true Mr. Cotton allows the same power to magistrates to punish all heretics, blasphemers, seducers, one as well as another. But what if it should fall out that his magistrates should declare themselves for the pope, or for the prelates, or for the presbyters—yea, or for some other way that is professed, and left it free for each man's conscience to worship as he believed, and to pay or not pay toward this or that worship or ministry according to his own persuasion, more or less, anything or nothing? Will not Mr. Cotton then plead that such magistrates themselves (apostatizing from the truth of God and turning enemies—as the pope clamors—to the holy church), I say, that such ought not only be accursed with the lesser and greater censures of suspension and excommunication but also punished with imprisonment, banishment, and death? Or, if they find the mercy of life and favor of an office (by some over-ruling providence), will not Mr. Cotton then plead that such magistrates ought to suspend their power, to hold their hands, and not to meddle until they be better informed? Into such poor, withered straws and reeds will the allowance of swords and staves Mr. Cotton here speaks of come to? Concerning the seats and saddles of great and settled maintenance of magistrates, the Discusser spake not, but heartily wisheth their maintenance as great and settled as he knows their labors and travels and dangers be: he spake only of ministers' great and settled maintenance.

Peace. O Truth, this is the apple of the eye, the true cause of so much combustion all the world over, especially Popish and Protestant!

Truth. Indeed this was the cause (as Erasmus told the Duke of Saxony) that Luther was so stormed at—because he meddled with the pope's crown and the monks' bellies. To obtain these warm and soft and rich seats and saddles (whoever stand or go on foot, or creep, or beg, or starve), the prelates' practices all ages know. Yea, and other practices of some of late who (with the evil steward providing wisely) first made sure of an ordinance of Parliament for tithes and maintenance before any ordinance for God Himself.[20] . . .

Peace. Yea, but saith Mr. Cotton, "I live not so."

Truth. One swallow makes not a summer: what others have done and do, and what practices have been and are for a forced maintenance (as firm and settled as ever was the parish maintenance of old England), hath been, to the shame of Christianity, too apparent. For Mr. Cotton himself, as I envy not the fatness of his morsels nor the sweetness of his cups, but wish him as large a purse as I believe he hath an heart and a desire to do good with it yet it hath been said that his case is no precedent, because what he loseth in the shire he gets in the hundred, and sits in as soft and rich a saddle as any throughout the whole country, through the greatness and richness of the merchandise of the town of Boston above other parts of the land. The truth is, there is no trial of the good or evil servant in this case until it comes to digging or begging—or the third way, *viz.*, of cozening of the great Lord and Master, Christ Jesus, by running to carnal means and carnal weapons to force men's purses for a rich and settled maintenance.

Truth. In the sad consideration of all which (dear Peace), let heaven and earth judge of the washing and color of this tenent. For thee, sweet heavenly guest, go lodge thee in the breasts of the peaceable and humble witnesses of Jesus that love the truth in peace! Hide thee from the world's tumults and combustions, in the breasts of thy truly noble children, who profess and endeavor to break the irony and insupportable yokes upon the souls and consciences of any of the sons of men.

Peace. Methinks (dear Truth) if any of the least of these deep charges be found against this tenent, you do not wrong it when you style it bloody. But since, in the woeful proof of all ages past, since Nimrod (the hunter or persecutor before the Lord), these and more are lamentably evident and undeniable, it gives me wonder that so many and so excellent eyes of God's servants should not espy so foul a monster, especially considering the universal opposition this tenent makes against God's glory and the good of all mankind.

Truth. There hath been many foul opinions with which

the old serpent hath infected and bewitched the sons of men (touching God, Christ, the Spirit, the church; against holiness, against peace, against civil obedience, against chastity), in so much that even sodomy itself hath been a tenent maintained in print by some of the very pillars of the Church of Rome. But this tenent is so universally opposite to God and man, so pernicious and destructive to both, that like the powder-plot, it threatens to blow up all religion, all civility, all humanity, yea, the very being of the world and the nations thereof at once.

Peace. He that is the father of lies and a murderer from the beginning, he knows this well, and this ugly blackamoor needs a mask and vizard.

Truth. Yea, the bloodiness and inhumanity of it is such that not only Mr. Cotton's more tender and holy breast, but even the most bloody Bonners and Gardiners have been forced to arm themselves with the fair shows and glorious pretenses of the glory of God and zeal for that glory, the love of His truth, the Gospel of Christ Jesus, love and pity to men's souls, the peace of the church, uniformity, order, the peace of the commonweal, the wisdom of the state, the king's, queen's and Parliament's proceedings, the odiousness of sects, heresies, blasphemies, novelties, seducers, and their infections: the obstinacy of heretics after all means, disputations, examinations, synods—yea, and after conviction in the poor heretic's own conscience. Add to these the flattering sound of those glossing titles: the godly magistrate, the Christian magistrate, the nursing fathers and mothers of the church, Christian kings, queens. But all other kings and magistrates (even all the nations of the world over, as Mr. Cotton pleads) must suspend and hold their hands, and not meddle in matters of religion, until they be informed, &c.

Peace. The dreadful righteous hand of God, the eternal and avenging God, is pulling off these masks and vizards that thousands—and the world—may see this bloody tenent's beauty.

Truth. But see, my heavenly sister and true stranger in this sealike, restless, raging world, see here what fires and swords are come to part us! Well, our meetings in the heavens shall not thus be interrupted, our kisses thus distracted, and our eyes and cheeks thus wet, unwiped. For me, though censured, threatened, persecuted, I must profess, while heaven and earth last, that no one tenent that either London, England, or the world doth harbor is so heretical, blasphemous, seditious, and dangerous to the corporal, to the spiritual, to the present, to the eternal good of all men as the bloody tenent (however washed and whited)—I say, as is the bloody tenent of persecution for cause of conscience.

VI

We comprehend what sort of radical Williams was—and how careless of his own interest—when we realize that in 1652, when he returned to London, Oliver Cromwell and the Independent clergy, headed by John Owen, could easily have embraced him, or he them, had he given the signal. His manuscript of *The Bloody Tenent yet More Bloody* was awaiting the final touches; Owen and his colleagues would welcome it, and Williams might well have aligned himself with these tolerationists, have been given an English charge, and never have come back to America (or at least not before the Restoration). The Dictator's liberalism, allowing freedom to all except those who extended the notion "beyond those bounds which the royal law of love and Christian moderation have set us in our walking one toward another," was so far beyond any rule of freedom Europe had yet envisaged that even a Roger Williams might have felt that the battle was won and have enlisted among Cromwell's friends.

However, there was a group of stubborn and serious men, most of whom had come out of Presbyterianism into a more radical Independency than John Owen's, who felt that the crux of real liberty was the abolition of the tithes —for until these compulsory payments were abrogated, the ecclesiastical order, even though tolerant of minor differences, remained something "established." Cromwell was hesitating. At the same time, under cover of the liberty he had thus far allowed, heresies judged pernicious by even the most liberal were appearing. John Owen, appointed by Cromwell to be Vice-chancellor of Oxford, persuaded Parliament (now composed mainly of Independents) to order the burning, on April 10, 1652, of an entire edition of *The Racovian Catechism*, the manual of Socinianism. At the same time, Owen and twenty-six Independent ministers petitioned Parliament to settle the English church on the basis of a state-supported institution, collecting the traditional tithes, with allowance for varieities.

Outside Parliament and Oxford—but inside the Army— were many who, with or without the help of typology, had arrived at conclusions as radical as Williams'. One of these, a Major William Butler, attempted in March of

1652 to bring pressure on the committee of Parliament, of which Cromwell was a member, by publishing four expostulatory papers. We do not know whether Williams was a friend of Butler, but we do know that he was intimate with the Vanes and with John Milton, all of whom agreed with Butler.

On March 30 Williams published a twenty-three-page pamphlet entitled, *The Fourth Paper, Presented by Major Butler, To the Honourable Committee of Parliament* (it is signed "r. w." and there is no mistaking the authorship.)[21] The booklet is obviously a hurried work, trying to make effective the not-yet-published manuscript. To shame Cromwell into acquiescence, Williams quotes him as saying "that he had rather that Mahometanism were permitted amongst us, than that one of God's children should be persecuted." The text stresses the point only touched on in the manuscript of the yet unpublished book, that ministers who bargain for a salary are utterly dissimilar from those whom Christ "sent" into the world. It succinctly proclaims that in "late years" God has made evident that civil magistracy is to be concerned only with civil affairs, and begs the committee to give the people absolute freedom, "so that no person be forced to pray nor pay, otherwise than as his soul believeth and consenteth." Once more reviewing the capriciousness of England's official changes of faith, Williams finds the revolutions of the Civil Wars proof that Christ will bless no national or state establishment. And, smuggled into this appeal is the basic argument:

That great pretense from the land of Canaan and the kings of Israel and Judah hath been in these late years proved but weak and sandy; and the Lord Jesus Christ

Himself to be the antitype of all those figures, the King and Head of all the Israel of God, forming, reforming His people.

Nevertheless, the news was leaking out that the committee of Parliament was not yet ready to abolish the tithes; Williams' great book was still in the press, and in a last desperate effort to tell Cromwell and the Independents what the issue was, he rushed through the printers in April *The Hireling Ministry None of Christs*. Thus, though both it and the pamphlet in defense of Major Butler appeared before *The Bloody Tenent yet More Bloody*, both were written after it.

The next month, while Williams and Milton were exchanging linguistic lessons (just as Clarke's book was appearing), Milton addressed a sonnet to Cromwell, telling him that peace has victories as well as war, beseeching him:

> Help us to save free conscience from the paw
> Of hireling wolves, whose Gospel is their maw.

But the Protector became occupied in foreign policy and the war with Holland; on April 29 the Independents— liberal men—decided that the tithes should still be collected. Radicals like Major William Butler, John Milton, Roger Williams were left to contemplate a revolution that stopped short of completion; but Williams, having struck three blows for the cause, could see that nothing more was to be expected from Cromwell. He had checked Coddington, and in February 1654 he sailed for America, once more armed with a safe conduct through Massachusetts. Again he voluntarily, deliberately, returned to the wilderness.

*The Hireling Ministry None of Christs, or a Discourse
touching the Propagating the Gospel of
Christ Jesus*
London. Printed in the Second Month. 1652.

THE EPISTLE DEDICATORY

*To all such honorable and pious hands whom the present
debate touching the propagating of Christ's Gospel
concerns;*

AND TO

All such gentle Bereans[22] *who with ingenious civility
desire to search whether what's presented concerning
Christ Jesus be so or no.*

All humble respective salutations:

IT BEING a present high debate (Honorable and Beloved) how the Gospel of Christ Jesus might more be prop-
agated in this nation, and being desired by eminent
friends to cast in my mite towards it, and having been engaged in several points in this nature in my former and
later endeavors against that bloody tenent of persecution
for cause of conscience, and also having been forced to
observe the doings of God and the spirits of men both in
old and New England as touching the church, the ministry, and ordinances of Jesus Christ—I did humbly apprehend my call from heaven not to hide my candle under a
bed of ease and pleasure, or a bushel of gain and profit,
but to set it on a candlestick of this public profession for
the benefit of others and the praise of the Father of all
lights and godliness. . . .

I humbly acknowledge (as to personal worth) I deal with men for many excellent gifts elevated above the common rank of men; yea, and for personal holiness (many of them) worthy of all true Christian love and honor, in which respects, when I look down upon myself, I am really persuaded to acknowledge my unworthiness to hold a candle or book unto them. And yet, if I give flattering titles unto men, my Maker (saith Elihu) would quickly take me away; and why therefore (since I have not been altogether a stranger to the learning of the Egyptians, and have trod the hopefulest paths to worldly preferments, which for Christ's sake I have forsaken), since I know what it is to study, to preach, to be an elder, to be applauded—and yet also what it is also to tug at the oar, to dig with the spade, and plow and labor and travel day and night amongst English, amongst barbarians—why should I not be humbly bold to give my witness faithfully, to give my counsel effectually, and to persuade with some truly pious and conscientious spirits rather to turn to law, to physic, to soldiery, to educating of children, to digging (and yet not cease from prophesying), rather than to live under the slavery—yea, and the censure (from Christ Jesus and His saints, and others also)—of a mercenary and hireling ministry?

To which end, my humble and hearty cry is to the Father of lights to plead with all His children of light effectually, so that they may look up, wonder, and say, "Am I a child of light? Is the Father of lights my Father, and the saints my fellow-brethren and scholars in Christ Jesus, the children of light also? Who make I then in dark places, like those that have been dead of old? What make

I amongst the graves and tombs, the livings, benefices, pro-
motions, stipends?"

Being desired by some loving friends to cast my mite
as to that heavenly proposition of propagating the Gospel
of Christ Jesus, I am humbly bold to propose these conclusions, and their consectaries following:

The civil state of the nations, being merely and essentially civil, cannot (Christianly) be called Christian states
after the pattern of that holy and typical land of Canaan.

The civil sword (therefore) cannot rightfully act either
in restraining the souls of the people from worship or in
constraining them to worship, considering that there is not
a title in the New Testament of Christ Jesus that commits
the forming or reforming of His spouse and church to the
civil and worldly power. . . .

No man ever did, nor ever shall, truly go forth to convert the nations, nor to prophesy in the present state of
witnesses against Antichrist, but by the gracious inspira-
tion and instigation of the Holy Spirit of God. . . .

I prejudice not an external test and call, which was at
first and shall be again in force at the resurrection of the
churches, . . . but in the present state of things, I cannot
but be humbly bold to say that I know no other true sender
but the most Holy Spirit. And when He sends, His messengers will go, His prophets will prophesy, though all the
world should forbid them. . . .

In the poor small span of my life, I desired to have been
a diligent and constant observer, and have been myself
many ways engaged: in city, in country, in court, in

schools, in universities, in churches, in old and New England; and yet cannot, in the holy presence of God, bring in the result of a satisfying discovery that either the begetting ministry of the Apostles or messengers to the nations, or the feeding and nourishing ministry of pastors and teachers (according to the first institution of the Lord Jesus), are yet restored and extant. . . .

The work of that commission (Matthew 28) was exercised and administered to the nations, as nations, and the world; but all our professed ministrations, former and latter, have been carried on (in a grand and common mystery) for the converting of a converted people. For, if we grant all Protestant nations to be Christians and so act with them in prayer as Christians and the children of God, how can we pretend to convert the converted and to preach unto them to convert them? One or other must be denied: to wit, that they are converted, or if unconverted, that we may offer up Christian and spiritual sacrifices with them. No herald, no ambassador sent to a city or army of rebels did ever (constantly least of all) perform such actions of state with those rebels which represents or renders them in a capacity of honest and faithful subjects. Oh, the patience and forbearance and long-suffering of the most high, whose eyes yet are as a flame of fire!

In their wages, whether by tithes or otherwise, they have always run in the way of an hire, and rendered such workmen absolute hirelings, between whom and the true shepherd the Lord Jesus puts so express and sharp a difference, so that in all humble submission I am bold to maintain that it is one of the grand designs of the most high to break down the hireling ministry, that trade, faculty, calling and living by preaching. And if all princes, states, parliaments, and armies in the world should join their heads and hearts and arms and shoulders to support it, yet being a part of Babel and confusion, it shall sink as a millstone from the angel's hand into the deeps forever.

He that makes a trade of preaching, that makes the cure of souls and the charge of men's eternal welfare a trade, a maintenance and living, and that explicitly makes a covenant or bargain—and therefore: no longer penny, no longer paternoster; no longer pay, no longer pray; no longer preach, no longer fast, &c.—I am humbly confident to maintain that the Son of God never sent such a one to be a laborer in His vineyard. Such notions spring not from the living and voluntary spring of the holy Spirit of God, but from the artificial and worldly respects of money, maintenance.

If the holy Scripture, the first pattern, and doleful experience may be judge, as an eminent person lately spake (upon occasion of a debate touching the conversion of the Indians), we have Indians at home—Indians in Cornwall, Indians in Wales, Indians in Ireland—yea, as to the point of true conversion and regeneration by God's Spirit, who can deny but that the body of this and of all other Protestant nations (as well as Popish) are unconverted, and (as formerly) ready to be converted and turned forward and backward, as the weather-cock, according as the powerful wind of a prevailing sword and authority shall blow from the various points and quarters of it.

By the merciful assistance of the most high, I have desired to labor in Europe, in America—with English, with barbarians—yea, and also I have longed after some trading with the Jews themselves (for whose hard measure I fear the nations and England hath yet a score to pay). But yet (as before), I cannot see but that the first and present great design of the Lord Jesus is to destroy the Papacy, in order to which two great works are first to be effected:

First, His calling of His people more and more out of the Babel of confused worships, ministries, &c., and the finishing of their testimony against the beast;

Secondly, the great sufferings and slaughters of the saints, upon occasion of which Christ Jesus in His holy wrath and jealousy will burn and tear the bloody whore of Rome in pieces.

We may hence see our great mistakes, both of ourselves and our forefathers, as to the pretended seed-plots and seminaries for the ministry: the universities of Europe and the universities of this nation. For although I heartily acknowledge that among all the outward gifts of God, human learning and the knowledge of languages and good arts are excellent, and excel other outward gifts as far as light excels darkness—and therefore that schools of humane learning ought to be maintained in a due way and cherished—yet notwithstanding, in *ordine ad ministerium* (as to the ministry of Christ Jesus), upon a due survey of their institutions and continual practices compared with the last will and testament of Christ Jesus, they will be found to be none of Christ's. . . .

As to the name "scholar"—although as to humane learn-

ing, many ways lawful—yet as it is appropriated to such as
practice the ministry, "have been at the universities" (as
they say), it is a sacrilegious and thievish title, robbing
all believers and saints, who are frequently in the testament of Christ styled disciples or scholars of Christ Jesus,
and only they as believers. And this title is so much theirs
that both men and women, believing, were called "scholars." . . .

As to their monkish and idle course of life, partly so
genteel and stately, partly so vain and superstitious, that
to set a finger in any pains or labor, it is a disgraceful and
an unworthy act. But the church is built upon the foundation of the Apostles and prophets, who were laborers,
fishermen, tentmakers, Jesus Christ (although the Prince
of life, yet) a poor carpenter, the chief cornerstone. And
I cannot but conceive that—although it should not please
the most holy and jealous God to stir up this renowned
state and their renowned Cromwell (the second) to deal
with our refined monasteries as that blessed Cromwell the
first did with the more gross and palpably superstitious in
Henry VIII his days[23]—yet in His time the Lord Jesus,
whose is all power in heaven and earth, will spew out these
seminaries of hirelings and mystical merchants out of His
mouth as He hath done their fathers, the superstitious and
bloody bishops before them.

Far be it from me to derogate from that honorable civility of training up of youth in languages and other humane
learning, whether in the city of LONDON or other towns
and cities. All that I bear witness against is the counter-
feiting, sacrilegious arrogating of the titles and rights
of God's saints and churches, which are the only schools

of the prophets; as also against their sacrilegious and superstitious "Degrees" (as they call them) in the profession of Divinity, as if they only knew divinity, godliness, holiness, and by such skill in godliness and by such "Degrees" might succeed the ancient Scribes and Pharisees in the uppermost seats in the synagogues and feasts, in reverend titles and salutations, as the only masters and teachers of religion and godliness—and all this in the way of the hireling, dividing the whole land for gain, so that there hath not been room (without some special and extraordinary privilege and license) for the poorest cottager to live in England out of the bishop's diocese and the priest's parish and payments.

For myself, I am sure of two things:

First, it is but little of the world yet that hath heard of the lost estate of mankind and of a Savior, Christ Jesus; and as yet the fullness of the gentiles is not yet come, and probably shall not, until the downfall of the Papacy. Yet,

Secondly, the ministry or service of prophets and witnesses, mourning and prophesying in sackcloth, God hath immediately stirred up and continued all along the reign of the beast and Antichrist of Rome.

This witness is (probably) near finished, and the bloody storm of the slaughter of the witnesses is yet to be expected and prepared for: but this, and the time, and many passages in Revelation 13, is controversial, and something like that of Christ's expected personal presence, the state of the New Jerusalem, the new heavens and earth, &c.

However, this is clear: that all that are betrusted with

spiritual or temporal talents must lay them out for their
Lord and Master His advantage.

The first grand design of Christ Jesus is to destroy and
consume His mortal enemy, Antichrist. This must be done
by the breath of His mouth in His prophets and witnesses.
Now the nations of the world have impiously stopped this
heavenly breath and stifled the Lord Jesus in His servants.
Now if it shall please the civil state to remove the state
bars set up to resist the holy Spirit of God in His servants
(whom yet finally to resist is not in all the powers of the
world), I humbly conceive that the civil state hath made
a fair progress in promoting the Gospel of Jesus Christ.

The *Summa totalis* of all the former particulars is this:
First, since the people of this nation have been forced
into a national way of worship, both Popish and Protestant
(as the wheels of time's revolutions, by God's mighty
providence and permission, have turned about), the civil
state is bound before God to take off that bond and yoke
of soul-oppression and to proclaim free and impartial
liberty to all the people of the three nations, to choose
and maintain what worship and ministry their souls and
consciences are persuaded of: which act, as it will prove an
act of mercy and righteousness to the enslaved nations, so
is it of a binding force to engage the whole and every interest and conscience to preserve the common freedom
and peace. However, an act most suiting with the piety
and Christianity of the holy testament of Christ Jesus.
Secondly, the civil state is humbly to be implored to

provide in their high wisdom for the security of all the respective consciences, in their respective meetings, assemblings, worshippings, preachings, disputings; and that civil peace and the beauty of civility and humanity be maintained among the chief opposers and dissenters.

Thirdly, it is the duty of all that are in authority, and of all that are able, to countenance, encourage, and supply such true volunteers as give and devote themselves to the service and ministry of Christ Jesus in any kind: although it be also the duty—and will be the practice of all such whom the Spirit of God sends upon any work of Christ's—rather to work as Paul did among the Corinthians and Thessalonians than that the work and service of their Lord and Master should be neglected.

Such true Christian worthies (whether endowed with humane learning or without it) will alone be found that despised model which the God of heaven will only bless: that handful of three hundred out of Israel's thirty-two thousand by whom the work of the God of Israel must be effected. And if this course be effected in the three nations, the bodies and souls of the three nations will be more and more at peace, and in a fairer way than ever to that peace which is eternal when this world is gone.

V The Long Winter of Retirement

I

THE LITTLE WORLD into which Williams came back, in 1654, demanded as much from him as had the great world of Cromwellian London. We need not here pursue the details of his administration as "president," nor his later efforts to exert an influence when he had become a superannuated, revered but often slighted, elder statesman. Cotton Mather termed these years "the long winter of his retirement," which was not so much a statement of fact as an opinion orthodox New England eagerly wanted to believe. Even so, there is this much truth in the phrase: the influence of Williams was henceforth curtailed to such power as he could wield in Rhode Island, and to such effect as he could work on the southern Indians. He had still to scramble for a living; he would not become a hireling minister, and after the Restoration in England, in 1660, he could figure that he was discharged from the wars, to await in calm expectation the fulfillment of prophecies—except when the impingement of colonial events aroused him to action, even if only to verbal response—while he awaited the solution of enigmas which he admitted were deeper than he had, in his confident youth, ever supposed.

In what mood he lived out this long winter of unretired retirement we have a full statement. He published it in the same April 1652 in which he issued *The Hireling Ministry*, while he was still preparing *The Bloody Tenent yet More Bloody*, but he had written it before he went to England. Sometime during his trading expeditions he received news that his wife was ill, and he knew that she, despite his efforts to instruct her, was as yet unlearned in the trials and tribulations God sends on His chosen. Out of the wilderness—probably at his station in Cocumcussot —he wrote her the sort of letter which he, and possibly she, would suppose to be an epistle of encouragement. When he published it, he called it *Experiments of Spiritual Life & Health,*[1] and he would not have put it to the press had he not taken it seriously. What effect it had on Mary Williams we know not; she, as he publicly informed her, was slow in her "writing" and therefore (presumably) in her comprehension of the written page. If she did get consolation from the manuscript, we might suspect that she would be less sustained by the printed text, with its dedications first to Lady Vane and then to Williams' old friend, "every truly Christian reader," but she by then was accustomed to the fact that Roger had to make the best of his rare opportunities in London.

The *Experiments* is, structurally, a conventional Puritan manual of self-analysis. The basic concern of every Puritan—as countless diaries reveal, as well as the more formal histories of Bradford, Winthrop, Johnson, Increase and Cotton Mather—was whether or not the chronicler himself was in a state of grace. Protestantism liberated men

from the treadmill of indulgences and penances, but cast
them on the iron couch of introspection. The orthodox New
England system, with its formula for receiving into the
church only visible saints, assumed that this process of
examination could be so successfully carried out that a
number of the more resolute would ultimately arrive at a
conviction of holiness, and would be able to demonstrate
it to the community—at least unto "visibility."

Williams had denied the covenant and the visible
church, and so might be supposed to have graver doubts
about the ascertaining of assurances. Yet, as we must
constantly remind ourselves, in theology this typologist
was completely orthodox. For him as for the casuists of
Massachusetts, the struggle for faith followed a norm;
there existed a standard chart on which the fluctuations
could be traced, against which the particular individual
could determine either his normality or his idiosyncrasy.
A thousand Puritan manuals in the century—the most explicit of them being Richard Baxter's *The Saints' Everlasting Rest* in 1650, but the most dramatic, John Bunyan's
Pilgrim's Progress in 1676—endeavored to systematize the
stages on life s way, so that the swimmer in midstream
might check his position against the approved course.

For Mary Williams her husband laid out such a chart.
First he told her what measures of spiritual life may be
authentic, despite the presence of doubts and "weaknesses"; then he set forth the ideal measures of grace in a
healthy spirit; and thirdly he enumerated the "spiritual
preservations"—those considerations which sustain one
after he (or she) has come to assurance yet thereafter is
overcome with doubts.

All this is thoroughly conventional, and there is very
little in Williams' manual to distinguish it from others.

But that little is important. There is, first of all, the dedication to the wife of Sir Henry Vane; the statesman who had befriended Mrs. Hutchinson in New England had become the leading advocate of absolute freedom in England (to whom Milton addressed the sonnet that answers his doubting encouragement to Cromwell), and in 1652 had already become an annoyance to the Protector.

Secondly, Williams' manual is tempted at every point, and seldom resists the temptation, to accent the phases of regeneration by a glance at his political and typological theory. This tendency comes inevitably to a climax in his endeavor to instruct his simple and adoring wife about his conception of history; this section, emerging in the last pages of his book, I quote. It makes an instructive commentary on his more resolutely controversial works: written in the wilderness, by the light of a fire, these thoughts are less assured as to the meaning of allegories, parables and similitudes than the young disputant had shown himself to Governor Winthrop. He had learned much in the wilderness, and things were not so clear as they had been in his Separatist youth; but as they had become more and more insubstantial, the certainty of a resolution outside this realm had become, if anything, more assured.

Experiments of Spiritual Life & Health, and their Preservatives. In which the weakest Child of God may get Assurance of his Spirituall Life and Blessednesse. And the Strongest may finde proportionable Discoveries of his Christian Growth, and the means of it

By Roger Williams of Providence in New-England
London, Printed in the Second Month, 1652

To the truly Honorable, the Lady Vane the younger

Madame: . . .

IT IS true, I have been sometimes pressed to engage in controversies, but I can really and uprightly say, my witness is on high how harsh and doleful the touch of those strings are—especially against such worthies both in old and New England in whom I joyfully before the world acknowledge (in many heavenly respects) a lively character and image of the Son of God. This broken piece is a breath of a still and gentle voice—none but the God of this world; and the men of this world can I lightly (at this turn) expect my opposites.

At other times I have been drawn to consider of the little flock of Jesus, His army, His body, His building, that for these many hundred years have been scattered, routed, and laid waste and desolate. At present, I only examine who are the personal and particular sheep of Jesus Christ, His soldiers, His living materials—though scattered, divided, and not composed and ordered at their souls' desire.

I confess, Madame, it was but a private and sudden discourse, sent in private to my poor companion and yokefellow, occasioned by a sudden sickness threatening death, into which and from which it pleased the Lord most graciously to cast and raise her.

The form and style I know will seem to this refined age too rude and barbarous. And the truth is, the most of it was penned and writ (so as seldom or never such discourses were) in the thickest of the naked Indians of America, in their very wild houses and by their barbarous fires, when the Lord was pleased this last year (more than ordinarily) to dispose of my abode and travel amongst them. And yet, is the language plain? It is the liker Christ's. Is the composure rude? Such was His outward beauty. Are the trials (seemingly) too close? Such is the two-edged sword of His most holy Spirit, which pierceth between the very soul and spirit, and bringeth every thought into the obedience of Christ Jesus. . . .

To every truly Christian reader:

As IT is in the earthly, so it is in the heavenly marriage of a poor sinner to His Maker: there useth first to pass a private kindling of love, and a private consent and promise (which sometimes are long), before the open solemnity and the public profession of a married life together. This is my present design (not to controvert the matters of public order and worship, but) to present some poor experiments of those personal excellencies of each true believing soul and spirit. . . .

'Tis true, all public and private Christian spirits pretend the spirit of holiness: yea, how great a part of the world pretend to be Christendom, the Christian world—that is, anointed with the Spirit of Christ Jesus? But was it death in Moses' rites to counterfeit that ceremonial and figurative ointment . . . what shall it be to counterfeit the spirit of life and holiness itself? What I believe, therefore (as David and Paul once spake), I freely speak: yea, who can but speak (saith Peter and John) the things they have seen and heard? I confess I spake these first but in a private letter in America, and thought not that the light in Europe should have seen them; but a twofold desire hath prevailed with me to expose these trials to the trying of all men:

1. The earnest desire of some godly friends;

2. Mine own desire of sowing a little handful of spiritual seed while the short minute of my seedtime (the opportunity of life) lasteth. . . .

'Tis true, the communion of saints is sweet and joyful, strong and powerful, eternally gainful and profitable; and holy and blessed is that spirit that makes the saints (who are the excellent of the earth) its delight. And after that blessed hour of the saints' uniting in one heart, one spirit, one worship—let all that love Christ Jesus mourn and lament, and breathe and pant: and yet the weakest and faintest lamb that comes but stealing in the crowd to touch the hem of the Lord Jesus His garment, that is content to be esteemed a dog and to wait for crumbs of mercy under the table of the Son of God—let them, I say, rejoice also, for He that hath begun that blessed work by His own free and eternal Spirit will, by the same His own holy arm, gloriously finish it.

I end (dear Christian) with the proposal of two Christian knots or riddles, not unsuitable to these present times and spirits:

First, why is the heart of David himself more apt to decline from God upon the mountain of joy, deliverance, victory, prosperity, than in the dark vale of the shadow of death, persecution, sickness, adversity?

Secondly, why is it, since God worketh freely in us to do and to will of His own good pleasure, that yet He is pleased to command us to work out our own salvation with fear and trembling? Let us humbly beg the finger (the Spirit) of the Lord to untie these knots for us!

My Dearest Love and Companion in this Vale of Tears:
THY LATE sudden and dangerous sickness, and the Lord's most gracious and speedy raising thee up from the gates and jaws of death—as they were wonderful in thine own and others' eyes, so I hope and earnestly desire they may be ever in our thoughts as a warning from heaven to make ready for a sudden call to be gone from hence: to live the rest of our short uncertain span more as strangers, longing and breathing after another home and country; to cast off our great cares and fears and desires and joys about this candle of this vain life that is so soon blown out; and to trust in the living God of whose wonderful power and mercy thou hast had so much and so late experience. . . .

Thy holy and humble desires are strong, but I know thy writing is slow, and that thou wilt gladly accept of this my poor help, which with humble thankfulness and praise to the Lord I humbly tender to His holy service and thine in Him.

I send thee (though in winter) an handful of flowers made up in a little posy for thy dear self and our dear children to look and smell on when I, as the grass of the field, shall be gone and withered.

A sharp and bitter pill to purge out spiritual corruption is a due and serious pondering of the nature of the justice of the most high, notwithstanding all the infinite sweetness of the ocean of His mercy, and notwithstanding all the colors and pretenses which we poor sinners invent to ourselves to hide from our eyes the greatness and dreadfulness and terrors of it. . . .

Objection: But John saith, "Perfect love casteth out fear."

I answer: The true love of God never casteth out the true fear of God but only that which is false and counterfeit, that which is the fear of a beast, of slaves, and devils. Hence it is that the spirit of the fear of the Lord was poured upon the Lord Jesus Himself. This fear is an holy awe or reverence proper to a true and heavenly ingenuous child of God, even (first and chiefly) to Christ Jesus, the elder brother (in a sense) of all the children of God. To cherish which holy fear of God, let us cast our eyes upon the fiery flashes of His severed justice revealed unto us in a threefold time—the time past, present, and to come:

From the time past, how dreadful is that we find of the rejection and ejection of so many gloriously heavenly spirits, the angels, tumbled down for their sin of pride from the height of heaven and their glorious attendance upon God to the depth of hell, in horrible slavery to everlasting sins and torments?

How dreadful was that doleful sentence upon the whole race of mankind for the sin of the first root, our first parents in paradise? How wonderful those plagues and destructions upon Pharaoh and the land of Egypt for their oppressing God's people?

And (before that) how fearful and horrible was that destruction and burning up of Sodom and Gomorrah and other cities with fire and brimstone from heaven? And (before both these) how wonderfully fearful and universal was the destruction of the whole world in that choking and all-o'erwhelming flood or deluge?

How fearful were the strokes of God's displeasure upon His own people of Israel in their many destructions and captivities? How fearful the rejection of ten tribes wholly swallowed up and lost for so many ages and generations? How lamentable were the destructions (and especially that by Titus and Vespasion) of the holy city, that glorious Jerusalem, in the slaughter and captivity of 1,100,000 Jews—men, women, and children? How fearful was the rejection of that whole nation of the Jews, ever since but a curse and scorn to all the rest of the nations of the world, to this day?

And (above all) who can but tremble at the impartial flames of God's justice on that green and innocent tree, His own and only begotten Son, Christ Jesus, when He stood surety in the room of sinners to make satisfaction for their transgressions? . . .

In the second place, let us cast our eyes abroad and behold the direful signs and tokens of God's severe justice executed at this present in the world. How lamentably do we see before our eyes the daily and continued effects of that first wrath upon mankind in so many sorrows of all sorts for the first transgression?

Let us consider of the great and constant reproach and misery over all the nations of the world by reason of God's righteous sentence in the division of so many tongues and languages.

"O, come and see," saith David, "what desolations the Lord hath wrought in the earth." How many hundred thousands of men, women, and children have of late years been swept away in the world by wars, famines, and pestilences? And since we are commanded to weep with them that weep:—O, that our heads were fountains and our eyes rivers of waters, that we might weep with Germany, weep with Ireland, yea, weep day and night with

England and Scotland (to speak nothing of other remote nations), in laying again and again to heart the strokes of God's most righteous judgments, in their most fearful slaughters and desolations.

The effects and marks of these most dreadful blows every eye is forced to see, but yet there are some strokes more fearful and yet not easily perceived: such are the righteous judgments of God giving up the nations of the world to so many horrible and blasphemous worships, idolatries, and superstitions. To speak nothing of whole nations and kingdoms that know not at all the true and living God, how cold and hard is that stone that lies upon the mouth of that wonderful grave of unbelief wherein the nation of God's choice and love, the Jews, lie buried and o'erwhelmed to this day? . . .

But (thirdly) from these two times of past and present, let us cast our eyes on the third, which is yet to come: as sure and wonderful will shortly be these two most wonderful and dreadful downfalls of those two so mighty monarchies (so great enemies to Christ Jesus)—the Turkish and the Popish—according to the prediction of the holy prophets! How fearful the effusion of the vials, in part fulfilled and yet to be poured forth in their season! And not a little wonderful is that mighty destruction of the nations, Gog and Magog, gathered as the sand of the sea against the camp of the saints of the holy city.

And (to come to the full period and final sentence of the most righteous judge of the whole world) with what horrors and terrors shall these heavens and earth pass away, this earth with the works thereof being consumed and burned up? How inconceivably direful will the last eternal judgment be, when two worlds of men (the former destroyed by water, and this by fire) shall appear before the most glorious tribunal of the Son of God? When all the most secret sins shall be brought to trial and an account shall be given for every idle word? . . .

Objection: But some say, "Can these sayings be any other than a parable or similitude? For is the Devil capable of any material fire such as now is grievous and painful to flesh and blood?"

I answer: Grant these sayings parabolical or similitudes, as also that of Dives and Lazarus: yet what are parables and similitudes but glasses to represent unto us in more plain and easy ways the holy truth and mind of God?

The kernel of truth is not the less sweet though wrapped up in the shells and husks. Beyond all question, therefore, Christ Jesus foretells most sure and inconceivable plagues to all that know not God and obey not His glorious Gospel: and by this worm that never dies, and this fire that never goes out, declares a torment to be inflicted upon both men and devils which shall be extreme like fire, which shall be universal upon the whole sinful creature, no part exempted—which shall also be eternal, never dying, never ending. Yet we may adore God's righteous judgments and (working out salvation with fear and trembling) make sure of a Jesus, a Savior, to deliver us from the wrath that is to come.

In the next place (my dear Love), let us down together by the steps of holy meditation into the valley of the shadow of death. It is of excellent use to walk often into Golgotha, and to view the rotten skulls of so many innumerable thousands of millions of millions of men and women like ourselves, gone, gone forever from this life, and being (as if they never had life nor being) as the swift ships, as the weaver's shuttle, as an arrow, as the lightning through the air.

It is not unprofitable to remember the faces of such whom we knew, with whom we had sweet acquaintance sweet society, with whom we have familiarly eaten and lodged, but now grown loathsome, ugly, terrible, even to their dearest, since they fell into the jaws of death, the king of terrors.

And yet they are but gone before us in the path all flesh must tread: how, then, should we make sure, and infinitely much, of a Savior who delivers us from the power and bitterness of death, and grave, and hell—who is a resurrection and life unto us, and will raise up and make our bodies glorious, like His glorious body, when He shall shortly appear in glory?

It is further of great and sweet use against the bitterness of death and against the bittersweet delusions of this world daily to think each day our last, the day of our last farewell, the day of the splitting of this vessel, the breaking of this bubble, the quenching of this candle, and of our passage into the land of darkness, never more to behold a spark of light until the heavens be no more.

Those three uncertainties of that most certain blow—to wit, of the time when, the place where, the manner how it shall come upon us and dash our earthen pitcher all to pieces—I say, the consideration of these three should be a threefold cord to bind us fast to an holy watchfulness for our departures, and a spur to quicken us to abundant faithfulness in doing and suffering for the Lord and His Christ. It should draw up our minds into heavenly objects and loosen us from the vexing vanities of this vain puff of this present sinful life.

Oh! how weaned, how sober, how temperate, how mortified should our spirits, our affections, our desires be when we remember that we are but strangers, converse with strange companies, dwell in strange houses, lodge in strange beds, and know not whether this day, this night, shall be our final change of this strange place for one far stranger, dark and doleful, except enlightened by the death and life of the Son of God?

How contented should we be with any pittance, any allowance of bread, of clothes, of friendship, or respect? How thankful unto God, unto man, should we poor strangers be for the least crumb, or drop, or rag vouchsafed unto us, when we remember we are but strangers in an inn, but passengers in a ship; and though we dream of long summer days, yet our very life and being is but a swift, short passage from the bank of time to the other side or bank of a doleful eternity?

How patient should our minds and bodies be under the crossing, disappointing hand of our all-powerful Maker, of our most gracious Father, when we remember that this is the short span of our purging and fitting for an eternal glory; and that when we are judged, we are chastened of the Lord, that we should not be condemned with the world?

How quietly (without the swellings of revenge and wrath) should we bear the daily injuries, reproaches, persecutings, from the hands of men who pass away and wither (it may be before night) like grass, or as the smoke on the chimney's top, and their love and hatred shall quickly perish?

Yea, how busy, how diligent, how solicitous should we be (like strangers upon a strange coast waiting for a wind or passage) to get despatched what we have to do before we hear that final call, "Away, away, let us be gone from hence."

How should we ply to get aboard that which will pass and turn to blessed account in our own country? How should we overlook and despise this world's trash which (as the holy woman going to be burned for Christ said of money) will not pass in heaven? How zealous for the true God, the true Christ, His praise, His truth, His worship: how faithful in an humble witness against the lies and cozening delusions of the father of lies, though gilded o'er with truth, and that by the hands of the highest or holiest upon the earth?

How frequent, how constant (like Christ Jesus our founder and example) in doing good (especially to the souls) of all men, especially to the household of faith— yea, even to our enemies—when we remember that this is our seedtime, of which every minute is precious, and that as our sowing is, must be our eternal harvest? For so saith the Spirit by Paul to the Galatians: "He that soweth to the flesh, shall of the flesh reap corruption or rottenness; and he that soweth to the spirit, shall of the spirit reap life everlasting."

II

Williams and Clarke got from the Council of State on October 6, 1652, a disallowance of Coddington's claim to an independent jurisdiction over the island that gives Rhode Island its name, Aquidneck as it was generally called. But negotiations for a full confirmation of the colony's charter were delayed by the Dutch War, so that Williams, at the end of his resources, came back in 1654, leaving Clarke to carry on in London (he had to carry on, in fact, through the Restoration, until in 1663 he brilliantly succeeded in procuring a royal charter from Charles II).

Williams came back to a community so torn with dissension as to be virtual anarchy; vigilante justice was about all that was left. He brought a letter from Sir Henry Vane, whom all Rhode Islanders reverenced, begging them to be peaceable, but the passions of mainlander against islander, and of factions within every town, were so exacerbated that not even Vane's exhortation could quiet them. In an effort to calm at least his own town, where he had most authority, Williams addressed the citizens in August, thus composing one of his noblest statements, at once a remarkable profile of the community, a record of his arduous service in London, and an expression of his ideal of a reasonable society in the wilderness. The letter had some effect in moderating passions and working out compromises, one of which was his election on September 12 to the office of "president." To us, however, the letter is most interesting as it shows in what spirit he who had penned the grandly "otherworld" conclusion to the *Experiments* now brought into focus the violence of this world's politics.

Letter to the Town of Providence, August 1654

Providence, August, 1654

Well-beloved friends and Neighbors:

I AM LIKE a man in a great fog. I know not well how to steer. I fear to run upon the rocks at home, having had trials abroad. I fear to run quite backwards, as men in a mist do, and undo all that I have been a long time undoing myself to do, *viz.*, to keep up the name of a people—a free people, not enslaved to the bondages and iron yokes of the great (both soul and body) oppressions of the English and barbarians about us, nor to the divisions and disorders within ourselves.

Since I set the first step of any English foot into these wild parts, and have maintained a chargeable and hazardous correspondence with the barbarians, and spent almost five years' time with the state of England to keep off the rage of the English against us, what have I reaped of the root of being the stepping-stone of so many families and towns about us but grief and sorrow and bitterness?

I have been charged with folly for that freedom and liberty which I have always stood for—I say, liberty and equality both in land and government. I have been blamed for parting with Moshassuck and afterwards Pawtuxet (which were mine own as truly as any man's coat upon his back) without reserving to myself a foot of land or an inch of voice in any matter more than to my servants and strangers. It hath been told me that I labored for a licentious and contentious people, that I have foolishly parted with town and colony advantages by which I might have preserved both town and colony in as good order as any in the country about us. This, and ten times more, I have been censured for, and at this present am called a traitor by one party against the state of England for not maintaining the charter and colony; and it is said I am as good as banished by yourselves, and that both sides wished that I might never have landed, that the fire of contention might have no stop in burning.

Indeed, the words have been so sharp between myself and some lately that at last I was forced to say they might well silence all complaints if I once began to complain, who was unfortunately fetched and drawn from my employment and sent to so vast a distance from my family to do your work of a high and costly nature for so many days and weeks and months together, and there left to starve, or steal, or beg, or borrow.

But blessed be God, who gave me favor to borrow one while and to work another, and thereby to pay your debts there and to come over with your credit and honor, as an agent from you who had, in your name, grappled with the agents and friends of all your enemies round about you.

I am told that your opposites thought on me, and provided—as I may say—a sponge to wipe off your scores and debts in England; but that it was obstructed by yourselves, who rather meditated on means and new agents to be sent over to cross what Mr. Clarke and I obtained.

But, gentlemen, blessed be God, who faileth not, and blessed be His name for His wonderful providences, by which alone this town and colony, and that grand cause of truth and freedom of conscience hath been upheld to this day. And blessed be His name who hath again quenched so much of our fires hitherto, and hath brought your names and His own name thus far out of the dirt and scorn, reproach, &c. . . .

Love covereth a multitude of sins. Surely your charges and complaints, each against other, have not hid nor covered any thing, as we use to cover the nakedness of those we love. If you will now profess not to have disfranchised humanity and love, but that, as David in another case, you will sacrifice to the common peace and common safety

and common credit that which may be said to cost you
something, I pray your loving leave to tell you that if I
were in your souls' case, I would send unto your opposites
such a line as this:

"Neighbors, at the constant request and upon the constant mediation which our neighbor, Roger Williams,
since his arrival hath used to us, both for pacification and
accommodation of our sad differences, and also upon the
late endeavors in all the other towns for an union, we are
persuaded to remove our obstruction, *viz.*, that paper of
contention between us, and to deliver it into the hands
of our aforesaid neighbor and to obliterate that order which
that paper did occasion. This removed, you may be
pleased to meet with, and debate freely, and vote in all
matters with us, as if such grievances had not been amongst
us." . . .

Gentlemen, I only add that I crave your loving pardon
to your bold, but true, friend,

Roger Williams

As president—an office with no defined powers, of little
dignity and no salary—Williams had to earn his own living, to keep Rhode Island at least coherent, and to prevent
the orthodox colonies from precipitating a destructive war
by their blustering and stupid Indian policy. In the midst
of these protracted crises, the town of Providence attempted, as an elementary precaution, to organize a militia.
Whereupon, in the name of Williams' own mighty principles of freedom of conscience, a number of pious citizens, most of them Baptists, objected.

Possibly Williams in the president's chair—even though
that was no more than a bench in his own house—now

viewed dissenters in a different light from that of the insurgent in Salem of 1635. In his own mind he could make out a case for his consistency since he had never, throughout the debate with Cotton, denied that civil magistrates could enforce purely civil regulations. But these conscientious objectors were making military service a religious scruple. I am inclined to think (with little evidence beyond a few letters and the conclusion of the *Experiments*) that the experience both of London and Rhode Island—his disillusionment with Cromwell and his weariness with the democracy—had deepened his sense of the impassable gulf between the perfection of the antitypical church and the miserable reality of the wilderness. At any rate, faced with the possibility that Providence would have no physical defenders, Williams, in January 1655, addressed to the pacifists and idealists one of his most pungent letters. It is perhaps the best known of all his writings, but the student of this volume will, I trust, consider it in the light of the particular circumstances as well as in that of the development herein recorded.

Letter to the Town of Providence, January 1655

Providence, January, 1655

THAT EVER I should speak or write a tittle that tends to such an infinite liberty of conscience is a mistake, and which I have ever disclaimed and abhorred. To prevent such mistakes, I shall at present only propose this case: There goes many a ship to sea, with many hundred souls in one ship,[2] whose weal and woe is common, and is a true picture of a commonwealth or a human combination or society. It hath fallen out sometimes that both Papists and

Protestants, Jews and Turks, may be embarked in one ship; upon which supposal I affirm that all the liberty of conscience that ever I pleaded for turns upon these two hinges: that none of the Papists, Protestants, Jews, or Turks be forced to come to the ship's prayers or worship, nor compelled from their own particular prayers or worship, if they practice any. I further add that I never denied that, notwithstanding this liberty, the commander of this ship ought to command the ship's course, yea, and also command that justice, peace, and sobriety be kept and practiced, both among the seamen and all the passengers. If any of the seamen refuse to perform their services, or passengers to pay their freight; if any refuse to help, in person or purse, towards the common charges or defense; if any refuse to obey the common laws and orders of the ship concerning their common peace or preservation; if any shall mutiny and rise up against their commanders and officers; if any should preach or write that there ought to be no commanders or officers because all are equal in Christ, therefore no masters nor officers, no laws nor orders, nor corrections nor punishments—I say, I never denied but in such cases, whatever is pretended, the commander or commanders may judge, resist, compel, and punish such transgressors according to their deserts and merits. This, if seriously and honestly minded, may, if it so please the Father of lights, let in some light to such as willingly shut not their eyes.

I remain studious of your common peace and liberty.

Roger Williams

Retiring from the presidency in 1657, Williams remained active in the government for a time, but, as the surviving letters show, he retired more and more into himself—especially after the Restoration of Charles II seemed to him, as it did to all Puritans, to mean the complete defeat of a once great expectation. In the 1660s Rhode Island and Connecticut fell into controversy over the area called the "Pequot lands" (around what is now Westerly). In 1670 agents of Connecticut resorted to invasion and forcible seizure. Williams gathered his old energies and wrote a letter to Major John Mason. Mason knew what inestimable services Williams had rendered in the Pequot War, when Mason commanded; though he knew that Williams had recoiled at his ruthlessness, and though he had no sympathy with Williams' ideas, the old soldier, who was a power in Connecticut, so respected his ancient companion that he exerted himself to check the invaders at Westerly.

It is entirely characteristic of Williams that, in order to persuade the Major, he should start at the beginning. The letter tells us, as no second-hand account could possibly do, how deeply the whole wilderness experience had entered into the being of Williams. It is one of the finest of American autobiographies; and it ends with a passage of organ-toned resignation that is one of the indubitably enduring achievements of Williams' prose.

Letter to Major John Mason, June 22, 1670

Providence, June 22, 1670

Major Mason—My honored, dear, and ancient friend, my due respects and earnest desire to God for your eternal peace:

I crave your leave and patience to present you with some few considerations occasioned by the late transactions be-

tween your colony and ours. The last year you were pleased,
in one of your lines to me, to tell me that you longed to see
my face once more' before you died. I embraced your
love, though I feared my old lame bones, and yours, had
arrested traveling in this world, and therefore I was and
am ready to lay hold on all occasions of writing, as I do at
present.

The occasion, I confess, is sorrowful, because I see yourselves, with others, embarked in a resolution to invade and
despoil your poor countrymen in a wilderness, and your
ancient friends of our temporal and soul liberties.

It is sorrowful, also, because mine eye beholds a black
and doleful train of grievous and, I fear, bloody consequences at the heel of this business, both to you and us.
The Lord is righteous in all our afflictions, that is a maxim;
the Lord is gracious to all oppressed, that is another; He is
most gracious to the soul that cries and waits on Him; that
is silver, tried in the fire seven times.

Sir, I am not out of hopes but that while your aged eyes
and mine are yet in their orbs, and not yet sunk down into
their holes of rottenness, we shall leave our friends and
countrymen, our children and relations, and this land, in
peace behind us. To this end, Sir, please you with a calm
and steady and a Christian hand to hold the balance and to
weigh these few considerations, in much love and due
respect presented:

First. When I was unkindly and unchristianly, as I believe, driven from my house and land and wife and children (in the midst of a New England winter, now about
thirty-five years past) at Salem, that ever honored Governor, Mr. Winthrop, privately wrote to me to steer my
course to Narragansett Bay and Indians, for many high and

heavenly and public ends, encouraging me from the freeness of the place from any English claims or patents. I took his prudent motion as a hint and voice from God, and waiving all other thoughts and motions, I steered my course from Salem (though in winter snow, which I feel yet) unto these parts, wherein I may say "Peniel," that is, I have seen the face of God.

Second. I first pitched, and began to build and plant at Seekonk, now Rehoboth, but I received a letter from my ancient friend, Mr. Winslow, then Governor of Plymouth, professing his own and others' love and respect to me, yet lovingly advising me, since I was fallen into the edge of their bounds and they were loath to displease the Bay, to remove but to the other side of the water, and then, he said, I had the country free before me and might be as free as themselves, and we should be loving neighbors together. These were the joint understandings of these two eminently wise and Christian governors and others in their day, together with their counsel and advice as to the freedom and vacancy of this place, which in this respect, and many other providences of the most holy and only wise, I called *Providence*.

Third. Sometime after, the Plymouth great sachem (Ousamaquin), upon occasion affirming that Providence was his land and therefore Plymouth's land, and some resenting it, the then prudent and godly Governor, Mr. Bradford, and others of his godly council, answered that if, after due examination, it should be found true what the barbarian said, yet having, to my loss of a harvest that year, been now (though by their gentle advice) as good as banished from Plymouth as from the Massachusetts, and I had quietly and patiently departed from them at their motion to the place where now I was, I should not be molested and tossed up and down again while they had breath in their bodies; and surely, between those, my friends of the Bay and Plymouth, I was sorely tossed for one fourteen weeks, in a bitter winter season, not knowing what bread or bed did mean, beside the yearly loss of no small matter in my trading with English and natives, being debarred from Boston, the chief mart and port of New England. God knows that many thousands pounds cannot repay the very temporary losses I have sustained. It lies upon the Massachusetts and me, yea, and other colonies joining with them, to examine with fear and trembling, before the eyes of flaming fire, the true cause of all my sorrows and sufferings. It pleased the Father of spirits to touch many hearts, dear to him, with some relentings; amongst which, that great and pious soul, Mr. Winslow, melted, and kindly visited me at Providence, and put a piece of gold into the hands of my wife for our supply.

Fourth. When the next year after my banishment, the Lord drew the bow of the Pequot War against the country, in which, Sir, the Lord made yourself, with others, a blessed instrument of peace to all New England, I had my share of service to the whole land in that Pequot business, inferior to very few that acted. . . .

However you satisfy yourselves with the Pequot conquest, with the sealing of your charter some weeks before ours,[3] with the complaints of particular men to your colony, yet upon a due and serious examination of the matter, in the sight of God, you will find the business at bottom to be,

First, a depraved appetite after the great vanities, dreams and shadows of this vanishing life, great portions of land, land in this wilderness, as if men were in as great necessity and danger for want of great portions of land as poor, hungry, thirsty seamen have, after a sick and stormy, a long and starving passage. This is one of the gods of New England, which the living and most high eternal will destroy and famish.

Second, an unneighborly and unchristian intrusion upon us, as being the weaker, contrary to your laws as well as ours, concerning purchasing of lands without the consent of the General Court. . . .

Third, from these violations and intrusions arise the complaint of many privateers, not dealing as they would be dealt with, according to the law of nature, the law of the prophets and Christ Jesus, complaining against others in a design in which they themselves are delinquents and wrong doers. I could aggravate this many ways with Scripture rhetoric and similitude, but I see need of anodynes (as physicians speak) and not of irritations. Only this I must crave leave to say, that it looks like a prodigy or monster that countrymen among savages in a wilderness—that professors of God and one Mediator, of an eternal life, and that this is like a dream—should not be content with those vast and large tracts which all the other colonies have (like platters and tables full of dainties), but pull and snatch away their poor neighbors' bit or crust; and a crust it is, and a dry, hard one, too, because of the natives' continual troubles, trials, and vexations.

Alas! Sir, in calm midnight thoughts, what are these leaves and flowers, and smoke and shadows, and dreams of earthly nothings, about which we poor fools and children, as David saith, disquiet ourselves in vain? Alas! what is all the scuffing of this world for, but "Come, will you smoke it?" What are the contentions and wars of this world about, generally, but for greater dishes and bowls of porridge, of which, if we believe God's Spirit in Scripture, Esau and Jacob were types? Esau will part with the heavenly birthright for his supping, after his hunting, for god belly; and Jacob will part with porridge for an eternal inheritance. O Lord, give me to make Jacob's and Mary's choice, which shall never be taken from me.

How much sweeter is the counsel of the Son of God, to mind first the matters of His kingdom; to take no care for tomorrow; to pluck out, cut off, and fling away right eyes, hands, and feet rather than to be cast whole into hell-fire; to consider the ravens and the lilies, whom a heavenly Father so clothes and feeds; and the counsel of His servant Paul, to roll our cares for this life also upon the most high Lord, steward of His people, the eternal God; to be content with food and raiment; to mind not our own, but every man the things of another; yea, and to suffer wrong, and part with what we judge is right, yea, our lives, and (as poor women martyrs have said) as many as there be hairs upon our heads, for the name of God and the Son of God His sake. This is humanity, yea, this is Christianity. The rest is but formality and picture, courteous idolatry and Jewish and Popish blasphemy against the Christian religion, the Father of spirits and His Son, the Lord Jesus. Besides, Sir, the matter with us is not about these children's toys of land, meadows, cattle government: but here, all over this colony a great number of weak and distressed souls, scattered, are flying hither from old and New England; the most high and only wise hath in His infinite wisdom provided this country and this corner as a shelter for the poor and persecuted, according to their several persuasions. . . .

Thus, Sir, the King's Majesty, though his father's and his own conscience favored Lord Bishops, which their father and grandfather King James, . . . sore against his will, also did, yet all the world may see, by his Majesty's declarations and engagements before his return, and his declarations and Parliament speeches since, and many suitable actings, how the Father of spirits hath mightily impressed and touched his royal spirit, though the bishops much disturbed him, with deep inclination of favor and gentleness to different consciences and apprehensions as to the invisible King and way of His worship. Hence he hath vouchsafed his royal promise, under his hand and broad seal, that no person in this colony shall be molested or questioned for the matters of his conscience to God, so he be loyal and keep the civil peace. Sir, we must part with lands and lives before we part with such a jewel. I judge you may yield some land and the government of it to us, and we, for peace sake, the like to you, as being but subjects of one king; and I think the King's Majesty would thank us for many reasons. But to part with this jewel, we may as soon do it as the Jews with the favor of Cyrus, Darius, and Artaxerxes. Yourselves pretend liberty of conscience, but alas! it is but self, the great god self, only to yourselves. The King's Majesty winks at Barbadoes, where Jews and all sorts of Christian and Antichristian persuasions are free, but our grant (some few weeks after yours was sealed, though granted as soon, if not before yours), is crowned with the King's extraordinary favor to this colony, as being a banished one, in which his Majesty de-

clared himself that he would experiment whether civil
government could consist with such liberty of conscience.
This his Majesty's grant was startled at by his Majesty's
high officers of state, who were to view it in course before
the sealing, but fearing the lion's roaring, they couched,
against their wills, in obedience to his Majesty's pleasure. ...

Sir, I lament that such designs should be carried on at
such a time, while we are stripped and whipped, and are
still under (the whole country) the dreadful rods of God,
in our wheat, hay, corn, cattle, shipping, trading, bodies,
and lives; when on the other side of the water, all sorts of
consciences (yours and ours) are frying in the bishops' pan
and furnace; when the French and Romish Jesuits, the
firebrands of the world for their god belly sake, are kindling at our back in this country, especially with the
Mohawks and Mohegans, against us, of which I know and
have daily information.

If any please to say, is there no medicine for this malady?
Must the nakedness of New England, like some notorious
strumpet, be prostituted to the blaspheming eyes of all
nations? Must we be put to plead before his Majesty, and
consequently the lord bishops, our common enemies? I
answer, the Father of mercies and God of all consolations
hath graciously discovered to me, as I believe, a remedy
which, if taken, will quiet all minds—yours and ours—will
keep yours and ours in quiet possession and enjoyment of
their lands, which you all have so dearly bought and purchased in this barbarous country, and so long possessed
amongst these wild savages; will preserve you both in the
liberties and honors of your charters and governments,
without the least impeachment of yielding one to another;
with a strong curb also to those wild barbarians and all the

barbarians of this country, without troubling of compromisers and arbitrators between you; without any delay, or long and chargeable and grievous address to our King's Majesty, whose gentle and serene soul must needs be afflicted to be troubled again with us. If you please to ask me what my prescription is, I will not put you off to Christian moderation or Christian humility, or Christian prudence, or Christian love, or Christian self-denial, or Christian contentment or patience. For I design a civil, a humane and political medicine which, if the God of Heaven please to bless, you will find it effectual to all the ends I have proposed. Only I must crave your pardon, both parties of you, if I judge it not fit to discover it at present. I know you are both of you hot; I fear myself, also. If both desire, in a loving and calm spirit, to enjoy your rights, I promise you, with God's help, to help you to them in a fair and sweet and easy way. My receipt will not please you all. If it should so please God to frown upon us that you should not like it, I can but humbly mourn and say with the prophet, that which must perish must perish. As to myself, in endeavoring after your temporal and spiritual peace, I humbly desire to say, if I perish, I perish. It is but a shadow vanished, a bubble broke, a dream finished. Eternity will pay for all.

Sir, I am your old and true friend and servant,

Roger Williams

The son of John Cotton, also named John, became minister at Plymouth, where he did not have a happy pastorate; he impresses us as one of those unfortunate youths overshadowed by the crushing image of a distinguished father. We get some insight into the terms in which the name of Williams must have figured at the Cottons' dinner table during the days of the *Bloudy Tenent* from the fact that nineteen years after the father's death the son should still have stored up in him the venom he discharged on Williams in December 1670. Cotton's letter does not survive, but we can make out the language from Williams' quotations. Williams was now stiff and crippled; that he any longer led an intellectual life—in the sense of reading new books or receiving fresh stimulations—may be doubted. But obviously, as both the letter to Mason and this to Cotton inform us, he brooded endlessly on the battles and fortunes he had passed. This letter constitutes a magnificent but solitary epilogue to the debate he had once conducted with the eyes of the world on him.

Letter to John Cotton of Plymouth, March 25, 1671

Providence, 25 March, 1671.

Sir—

Loving respects premised. About three weeks since, I received yours, dated in December, and wonder not that prejudice, interest, and passion have lifted up your feet thus to trample on me as some Mahometan, Jew, or Papist, some common thief or swearer, drunkard or adulterer, imputing to me the odious crimes of blasphemies, reproaches, slanders, idolatries, to be in the Devil's kingdom, a graceless man, and all this without any Scripture, reason, or argument which might enlighten my conscience as to any error or offense to God or your dear father. I have now much above fifty years humbly and earnestly begged of God to make me as vile as a dead dog in my own eye so that I might not fear what men should falsely say or cruelly do against me; and I have had long experience of his merciful answer to me in men's false charges and cruelties against me to this hour.

My great offense (you so often repeat) is my wrong to your dear father—your glorified father. But the truth is, the love and honor which I have always showed (in speech and writing) to that excellently learned and holy man, your father, have been so great that I have been censured by divers for it. God knows that, for God's sake, I tenderly loved and honored his person (as I did the persons of the magistrates, ministers, and members whom I knew in old England, and knew their holy affections, and upright aims, and great self-denial, to enjoy more of God in this wilderness); and I have therefore desired to waive all personal failings, and rather mention their beauties, to prevent the insultings of the Papists or profane Protestants, who used to scoff at the weaknesses—yea, and at the divisions—of those they used to brand for Puritans. The holy eye of God hath seen this the cause why I have not said nor writ what abundantly I could have done, but have rather chose to bear all censures, losses, and hardships.

This made that honored father of the Bay, Mr. Winthrop, to give me the testimony not only of exemplary diligence in the ministry (when I was satisfied in it), but of patience also, in these words in a letter to me: "Sir, we have often tried your patience, but could never conquer it." My humble desire is still to bear not only what you say but, when power is added to your will, an hanging or burning from you, as you plainly intimate you would long since have served my book had it been your own, as not being fit to be in the possession of any Christian.

Alas! Sir, what hath this book merited above all the

many thousands full of old Romish idols' names, and new
Popish idolatries, which are in Christians' libraries and
use to be alleged in testimony, argument, and confutation?

What is there in this book but presseth holiness of heart,
holiness of life, holiness of worship, and pity to poor sinners, and patience toward them while they break not the
civil peace? 'Tis true, my first book, *The Bloudy Tenent*,
was burnt by the Presbyterian party (then prevailing);
but this book whereof we now speak (being my reply to
your father's answer) was received with applause and
thanks by the army, by the Parliament, professing that,
of necessity—yea, of Christian equity—there could be no
reconciliation, pacification, or living together but by permitting of dissenting consciences to live amongst them. . . .
And, Sir, I add, if yourself, or any in public or private,
show me any failing against God or your father in that
book, you shall find me diligent and faithful in weighing
and in confessing or replying in love and meekness. . . .

You are pleased to count me excommunicate; and therein
you deal more cruelly with me than with all the profane,
and Protestants and Papists too, with whom you hold communion in the parishes, to which (as you know) all are
forced by the bishops. And yet you count me a slave to
the Devil, because, in conscience to God and love to God
and you, I have told you of it. But, Sir, the truth is (I
will not say I excommunicate you, but) I first withdrew
communion from yourselves for halting between Christ
and Antichrist—the parish churches and Christian congregations. Long after, when you had consultations of killing
me but some rather advised a dry pit of banishment, Mr.
Peters advised an excommunication to be sent me (after
the manner of Popish bulls); but this same man, in Lon-

don, embraced me, and told me he was for liberty of conscience, and preached it. . . .

Sir, you tell me my time is lost because (as I conceive you) not in the function of ministry. I confess the offices of Christ Jesus are the best callings; but generally they are the worst trades in the world, as they are practiced only for a maintenance, a place, a living, a benefice. God hath many employments for His servants. Moses forty years and the Lord Jesus thirty years were not idle, though little be known what they did as to any ministry; and the two prophets prophesy in sackcloth and are Christ Jesus His ministers, though not owned by the public ordinations. God knows, I have much and long and conscientiously and mournfully weighed and digged into the differences of the Protestants themselves about the ministry. He knows what gains and preferments I have refused in universities, city, country, and court, in old England and something in New England, to keep my soul undefiled in this point and not to act with a doubting conscience. God was pleased to show me much of this in old England; and in New, being unanimously chosen teacher at Boston (before your dear father came, divers years) I conscientiously refused and withdrew to Plymouth, because I durst not officiate to an unseparated people, as, upon examination and conference, I found them to be. At Plymouth, I spake on the Lord's days and weekdays, and wrought hard at the hoe for my bread (and so afterward at Salem) until I found them both professing to be a separated people in New England (not admitting the most godly to communion without a covenant) and yet communicating with the parishes in old by their members repairing on frequent occasions thither.

Sir, I heartily thank you for your conclusion—wishing

my conversion and salvation, without which, surely, vain
are our privileges of being Abraham's sons, enjoying the
covenant, holy education, holy worship, holy church or
temple; of being adorned with deep understanding, miraculous faith, angelical parts and utterance; the titles of
pastors or apostles; yea, of being sacrifices in the fire to
God.

> Sir, I am unworthy (though desirous to be),
> Your friend and servant,
> *Roger Williams*

III

From the beginning to the end, Williams was always in
his theological creed an orthodox Calvinist; the six fundamentals he recited to Cotton (page 115) remained truly
fundamental, and the authority of the Bible was absolute.
The only heresy that separated him from Cotton and the
orthodox was his typology, but once he substituted that
different premise, he reasoned very much as they did.
Like them, or even more than were they, he was a "strict
constructionist" of Scripture. He wanted the state to
enforce the same moral regulations that were on the
statute books of Massachusetts; but he could not see how
a government in the modern dispensation, without the
sanctions given to a type, could achieve such efficiency in
administration as was Israel's by divine appointment:
"Adultery," he wrote the young Winthrop, "is a fire which
will root out, but the gentiles, the nations of the world,
will never be proved capable of such laws and punishments as that holy nation, bred up and fed with miracu-

lous dispensations, were fit for." So in the 1670s Williams was caught in a stick he himself had cleft when the Quakers, availing themselves of Rhode Island's freedom, poured in, not only disturbing the civil peace but preaching a theology which shocked Williams as profoundly as his typology had scandalized John Cotton.

Modern admirers who try to fit Williams into their pattern of liberality regard his opposition to the Quakers as a blot on his record, as a failing of senility. Thus they betray an utter failure to comprehend Williams' mind. We need to remind ourselves that the Quakers who, in those first intoxicating days, followed George Fox and Edward Burrough were not the sober citizenry of today but a mob of crassly assertive, ignorant and reckless fanatics. They preached an absolute authority of the inner light, of a direct inward communication from on high, which to a Biblicist like Williams—for whom the personal Jesus, crucified in Jerusalem, was the central and decisive fact in history—seemed an even more disastrous subordination of revelation to mere man-made fantasy than the political covenant taught in Boston. In his lame old age, Williams fought the Quakers for the same reason that he had fought Cotton in his manhood: any hasty generalization, arrived at without fear and trembling, without punctilious respect for the Word—whether it be a wrong interpretation of the covenant or the prompting of an impulse called the inward light—crystallizes into self-righteousness. Once the typological insight is granted, the Bible becomes an instrument for the shattering of self-esteem—wherefore Williams was not, nor could he ever have become, a liberal in the Jeffersonian or Utilitarian sense.

There was, on the other hand, nothing of the mystic or

pantheist about him: the Bible was law, the physical universe was divinely governed but not infused with divinity. He was simply aghast that Fox should speak of saints as indissolubly united with the essence of God, for "the essence or being of the immortal, invisible, infinite, eternal, omnipotent and omniscient, and wise, we know no more than a fly knows what a king is." To him, this sort of self-infatuation was bound to become what later generations call solipsism. He was, at heart, so much the Puritan that he demanded first of all a respect for the objective reality of the created universe (even though it be a vale of tears), and distrusted with every fiber of his being a theology of influx which was certain to deny the tangibility of existence.

Let this proud Fox, or any of the stoutest lions or lionesses amongst them, look but a few minutes upon the glorious sun in the heavens, and then tell us how their eyes do: and yet thus like proud and prattling children do they make a noise about their bibs and aprons and muckingers, and how they are one with God in His being and essence.

The all-important distinction between creation and immanence comes out, for instance, in such a cry as this:

It is not enough for sun, moon, and stars, and men to be enlightened by His infinity, but they must be God Himself, and light itself, in the sense, because God is light.

Thus it seemed to Williams—here I think the modern spirit should heed him—that whoever speaks with the accents of spiritual finality, whether an Endecott or a Fox (even though Fox renounces the use of force), is a danger to the spirit. Williams' greatest insight is into the corrosive effects not of sin but of virtue. The worst enemy of the soul is not the profane antagonist or persecutor, but the soul's rectitude. Every gathering of the righteous into a society of purity, in which the Bible becomes only a support to the aims of the community, is a fatal temptation. The Quakers seemed the most insidious form of this temptation yet let loose on a susceptible people.

His hostility may have been aggravated by the fact that many in Rhode Island who had made life miserable for him—notably Coddington—became converts. The situation was unendurable in 1672 when George Fox himself came to Rhode Island. Williams was always convinced that rational argument could settle everything, and so sent to Fox a fourteen-point challenge to debate. The letter reached Newport after Fox had left; Williams rowed all day from Providence to Newport, to confront in the morning not Fox but three of Fox's disciples, John Stubbs, John Burnet and William Edmundson. The first two, Williams says, could at least cite Scripture, but Edmundson was "very ignorant in the Scripture or any other learning," was a loud-mouthed braggart who "would often vapor and preach long, and when I had patiently waited till the gust was over, and began to speak, then would he stop my mouth with a very unhandsome clout of a grievous interruption: so that sometimes I was forced to play the moderator, and to protest that such practices were against the sober rules of civility and humanity." Amid the pandemonium of this "debate," the old man was still he who had written the *Key*:

We English were ourselves at first wild and savage Britons; God's mercy had civilized us, and we were now come into a wild and savage country, without manners, without courtesy, so that generally, except you begin with a "What cheer" or some other salutation, you had as good meet an horse or a cow. And hath not the Quaker spirit been such a spirit amongst us?

The audience, mostly Baptists and Quakers, heckled him with cries of "old man, old man," and whispered, after he had on the first day shouted himself hoarse in order to get any hearing, that he was drunk. The exhibition went on for three days in Newport, August 9 to 12, and then moved to Providence for another performance on August 17. When it was over, Williams sat down and wrote a report, with all that relentless passion for detail which never spared himself or his enemies anything—and today does not spare his readers. The account was published in Boston in 1676; there, in the strange revolutions of time, a work of Roger Williams was enthusiastically welcomed.

The title is a pun that arose by accident out of the first day of confusion. Edmundson suddenly said that Williams was insulting the holy Fox and the sainted Burrough by deriding "Fox in his Burrough." Williams had little aptitude for wit, and at first resented the idea that he should be accused of so vulgar a trick. George Fox (1624-1691) had summoned Edward Burrough out of Presbyterianism in 1652, when Burrough was seventeen; following his master, Burrough became an itinerant preacher and a prolific pamphleteer (he published some ninety titles, either alone or in collaboration with Fox). It was Burrough who pushed his way into the presence of Charles II and so terrified that feckless monarch that a royal letter was sent to Boston to stop the execution of Quakers. But Burrough profited no further from the king's favor; in 1662 he was thrown into

Newgate (out of which the Anabaptist had written the pages to which Cotton had been foolish enough to reply) and was so barbarously treated that he died a martyr, if ever any was, to the cause of conscience.

By the lights of today we may feel that Williams surrendered all sense of taste by adopting the pun, but in that sort of taste Williams was always deficient. By the time he wrote his narrative, it seemed to him a gift of providence. "It was also God's overruling hand that William Edmundson should so upbraid me and first put the conceit and thought of such a consideration into me, which I apprehend as *Digitus Dei,* the finger of God directing and pointing me to so proper and pertinent an use and application." The book tells much of Rhode Island history, because a good part of the interchange became mere name-calling—Williams giving as good as he got. Unless one is interested in these local spats, most of the book is today unreadable. And yet there are wonderful passages in it, and no understanding of Williams will be complete unless it is taken fully into account.

Of course, all the time he opposed the Quakers, Williams never for a moment suggested taking civil action against them. Even so, the three Quakers pressed him hard by accusing him of treason to his own principles:[4] "You mind me again of my books against persecution, and yet myself a persecutor of my peaceable neighbors." Thus the impression comes down to a heedless posterity that he went back on *The Bloudy Tenent.* Actually, where he was most in the toils, and where he spoke out most honestly and courageously—where he exhibited in public his innermost secret —was when he had to explain on the one hand why he believed passionately in the historical, the crucified and risen

Christ, and yet on the other why he would not, or could
not, join in any organized Christian society.

George Fox Digg'd out of his Burrowes, Or an Offer of
Disputation On fourteen Proposalls made this last
Summer 1672 (so call'd) unto G. Fox then present
on Rode-Island in New-England, by R. W.

Boston, 1676

Now to the proof of my second position, which was:
"That their Christ was not the true Lord Jesus Christ."

Here I prayed their patience to suffer me to tell them
that they were not Christians nor professors of Christian
religion: they might (with Jews and Turks and Papists)
profess one God, yet Christians they could not be. But as
the true Lord Jesus told us, many false Christs and false
prophets should come, who like mountebanks instead of
true physicians, and false and counterfeit money instead
of true, should with Satan's power and policy pass up and
down and deceive peoples and nations; so I must affirm
and declare that for their parts they had cut off the head
of the Christian religion, and they had set up a false Christ,
a false king, an usurper in His stead: they had like Michal
put a wooden image upon a pillow of goat's hair in David's
bed, but David himself was gone, the true David, the true
Lord Jesus Christ was not to be found amongst them. This
I spake expressly and they did hear me awhile. . . .

I affirmed their Christ was but half a Christ, a light, an
image or picture or fancy of a Christ, made up of the God-
head and their flesh. I said they had set up a Christ within
them which was but an imagination, an image, a Christ in

the mystical notion, but in reality nothing. For as the Papists make use of the name Christ, and the Pope saith he is Christ's vicar and lieutenant, and he doth all for Christ—and the Jesuits (soaring above all Christians) pretend the name of Jesus—and yet the Protestant witnesses have made it to appear that in many respects the Papists are infinitely against both Christ and Jesus, and so are not Christians but Antichristians. So I told them did they: they blew a trumpet for Christ Jesus, God in man, the everlasting Father, that we are bone of His bone and flesh of His flesh, that He was so born at Bethlehem and died at Jerusalem. Yet all these fair flourishes and colors are but as an English flag in a Spanish or Dutch or any other Christ is spiritual—that Christ, God and man, is within us, enemy's bottom. For do not all their books declare that that His birth, His life, His death, His burial, His resurrection, His ascension are wrought within us, so that like the oracles of Apollo and the echoes of the Jesuits, the Quakers say, "Christ was born at Bethlehem and died at Jerusalem," but intend in truth and reality no other birth nor life nor death but what may be extant and wrought in the heart of man. . . .

I told them I acknowledged Christ within as much as any of them—and infinitely more—for I did confess that every believing soul did bring home and apply the power and virtue of Christ's birth, and life and death. . . . I said there was a nearer union between Christ Jesus and a soul believing on Him than between a man and his wife, and between the soul and body. That union is earthly and dissolving: but that between Christ Jesus and the believer, it is eternal in God's decrees and counsels; it is temporary in God's calling of His chosen out of the world, to repentance and belief in the Mediator Christ Jesus, and it is perpetuated and continues to eternity.

I told them that (as the holy Scripture saith) they preached not Christ Jesus but themselves—yea, they preached the Lord Jesus to be themselves; that whatever were their pretenses (as the Papists) of God and Christ and holiness and mortification, yet they held not the head (as Scripture speaks), and if their head be but a painted and an imaginary head, they are but a painted and imaginary body. Their sun of righteousness they talk of is but a sun painted upon a sign or wall, which is not the true sun but the picture of the sun of righteousness.

I told them they set up this Christ within, opposite to Christ without, as opposites and contraries, denying and destroying one another: for as it is with a king and his palace, if his person be without, his person at that time is not within, though he be within by his right, authority, and influence; if his person be within the palace at that time, it is not without. But the most clear truth is, though these subtle Foxians sometimes speak of a Christ without that died at Jerusalem agreeing with the Christ within, yet they presently declare their meaning to be mystical. For ask them but these two questions, and if they make any answer, you will see the cheat, the equivocation and the mystery of iniquity in it:

1. Do they not hold the light within every man to be all, to do all, and to suffer all within which the Christ without is, or did or suffered without?

2. Ask them now what is become of this man, this person that thus suffered at Jerusalem, and they are forced to confess he is within, and can give no other account of

Him, as they answered to me at Newport the last day of the conference. . . .

I observe, this foolish Fox (for all his hiding craft) is here found out: he professeth (against his will and heart) a Christ that died at Jerusalem, and therefore is forced to name a Christ without. But when the hole and Burrough is digged, the Fox is found: for examine what is this Christ without? Is He that literal, real and material person, the Son of Mary (as all professing Christ's name generally agree)? Is this He whom the Quakers acknowledge to have lived and died at Jerusalem? And do they intend a material cross, a literal death, a literal and real Jerusalem? Some of them will say yes, but therein give the lie to others of themselves—and also to the rest of their own story—in acknowledging no other Christ but such as is in every man. Such a Christ as really and bodily died at Jerusalem, they scorn and hate and fly from as the devils did, crying out "What have we to do with thee, Jesus thou Son of the most high God; art thou come to torment us before the time?" . . . Fox saith, "This Jesus Christ without and within is Jesus Christ yesterday and today, and the same forever." Therefore, in the logic or reason of this brute, Christ had no body that was born at Bethlehem or died at Jerusalem, for He was born yesterday, and today, and He is born forever; He died yesterday, and He dies today, and He dies forever, which is a most heavenly truth relating to God's purposes, Christ's merit, and to forefathers', our present times, and such as yet must be born and follow after us.

But such mystical and figurative Scriptures (which are in themselves like Sampson's lion and riddle), through Satan's policy and the proud simplicity of these simple

Foxes, are made the common holes and Burroughs where
you may be sure to find them; just like the Jesuits (whose
cousins, if not brethren of one belly of hell, they are),
who usually confound clear Scriptures with spiritual and
mystical illusions, and fly from distinctions and openings
necessary in places more dark, figurative, and allegorical. . . .

Although I desired to finish all the first seven positions
that day, and offered once or twice to proceed, yet William Edmundson (especially) upbraided me that I kept
them long and that I proved nothing, and upon a sudden
a violent, tumultuous, disorderly wind or spirit filled all his
sails, so that he rose up and fell into a downright speech or
sermon to the people and auditory. And first he declared
how notoriously I had wronged them in laying and publishing so many false, and some of them dangerous,
charges against them. 2. And how they had been so long
patient towards me and suffered me to produce so many allegations out of George Fox his book, and yet they speak
nothing for me, but George Fox his words cleared him
from all my unjust challenges and charges. 3. He appealed
to the people, how willing they had showed themselves to
own the Scriptures and to have all their teachings and
differences tried by the Scriptures. 4. He fell upon the two
hinges of all the Quakers' common discourses:

First, an invective against the priests, false teachers,
false apostles, who had got on the sheep's clothing and
sold the words of Scripture for their game and lucre; and
he amplified this much, how all their care and study was
to get a good living or benefice of fifty, sixty, a hundred, or
two hundred pounds a year. . . .

The second part of his sermon was (as usually it is of

all their sermons) an extolling and magnifying of that light which, he said, had appeared to him, which he advanced as the principle and the foundation, the light &c. He added how they had left all the glory and pleasures of the world for this light: and how they had endured and suffered much for preaching this light to ungodly and ungrateful men, who had ill requited them. For their message and work was only to bring good news unto them, to tell them that they should be free from sin, and have Christ Jesus live and dwell in them.

I kept silence until this famous apostle and preacher of Christ Jesus had done this speech or sermon, which he said he was moved in his heart to make unto them and (as he often said) to give an account of his faith, which he performed with very great zeal and fervency, both of mind and body.

I had thought then to have spoke, but immediately John Stubbs stood up, being moved (as he said) to declare his mind and thoughts unto the people also, and so he began a large oration, speech or sermon also. . . . I heard him also patiently, and gave no interruption (as he twice openly confessed that I had not interrupted them); but when he had finished his sermon and I had gained a little calm and liberty of speech, immediately before I could finish one sentence that pragmatical and insulting soul, William Edmundson, stopped and interrupted me, so that I openly complained of incivility and inhumanity: that hearing patiently their two sermons, they were sat down, and common reason said that it was my turn to speak, and everybody desired what answer I could frame to hear it, that then I should be disturbed and stopped was no way befitting the societies of civil and moral men. I then answered that those very sermons or orations which they had now made to the people were so far beneath the merit of an answer to them that they ministered and afforded to me a mighty invincible argument that the Spirit of God was not the author of them. For we all knew that the Spirit of God was most purely rational, and a Spirit of pure order, and did not prompt or move men to break hedges and leap over one ordinance into another. We were engaged in a mutual conference and disputation, we were in the midst of it; how came we then to fall into popular orations and sermons? Is it comely when persons are disputing to fall upon our knees and answer an argument with a prayer (as is a frequent practice with the Quakers)? Is it proper to break off prayer and fall to disputing, or out of disputation into preaching? . . .

I said I would contract my thoughts and speak at present only a little of His kingly power and office; and I plainly denounced that they were all notoriously guilty of high treason against the King of kings, the Lord Jesus, yea as far as in them lay they robbed Him of His crown and life and all.

In particular I told them I had abundant proof there ready to bring forth from George Fox's book that he and his associates denied (yea, all of them) that visible kingdom and church and institutions which He as King over all his subjects hath sovereign right unto, and most faithfully and wisely ordained to continue until His coming again. . . .

Upon this (as I remember) there fell out some words between my opposites and some of the people called Baptists; but some of them (especially John Stubbs) demanded of me why I thus charged them and was myself so guilty, not living in church ordinances myself?

I answered that it was one thing to be in arms against the King of kings and His visible kingdom and administration of it, and to turn off all to notions and fancies of an invisible kingdom and invisible officers and worships, as the Quakers did; another thing, among so many pretenders to be the true Christian army and officers of Christ Jesus, to be in doubt unto which to associate and to lift ourselves.

After all my search and examinations and considerations, I said, I do profess to believe that some come nearer to the first primitive churches and the institutions and appointments of Christ Jesus than others, as in many respects, so in that gallant and heavenly and fundamental principle of the true matter of a Christian congregation, flock, or society, *viz.*, actual believers, true disciples and converts, living stones, such as can give some account how the grace of God hath appeared unto them and wrought that heavenly change in them. I professed that if my soul could find rest in joining unto any of the churches professing Christ Jesus now extant, I would readily and gladly do it—yea, unto themselves whom I now opposed.

Epilogue

The Significance of Roger Williams for the American Tradition

For the subsequent history of what became the United States, Roger Williams possesses one indubitable importance, that he stands at the beginning of it. Just as some great experience in the youth of a person is ever afterward a determinant of his personality, so the American character has inevitably been molded by the fact that in the first years of colonization there arose this prophet of religious liberty. Later generations may not always have understood his thought; they may have imagined that his premises were something other than the actual ones, but they could not forget him or deny him. He exerted little or no direct influence on theorists of the Revolution and the Constitution, who drew on quite different intellectual sources, yet as a figure and a reputation he was always there to remind Americans that no other conclusion than absolute religious freedom was feasible in this society. The image of him in conflict with the righteous founders of New England could not be obliterated; all later righteous men would be tormented by it until they learned to accept his basic thesis, that virtue gives them no right to impose on others their own definitions. As a symbol, Wil-

254

liams has become an integral element in the meaning of American democracy, along with Jefferson and Lincoln.

However, the student of Williams' own writings will, I trust, perceive that great as has been his symbolic role, he himself was thinking on a deeper plane than that which simply recognizes religious liberty as a way for men to live peaceably together. He was not a rationalist and a utilitarian who gave up the effort to maintain an orthodoxy because he had no real concern about religious truth, but was the most passionately religious of men. Hence he is an analyst, an explorer into the dark places, of the very nature of freedom. His decision to leave denominations free to worship as they chose came as a consequence of his insight that freedom is a condition of the spirit.

Of course, as these selections show, this statement needs to be qualified by the observation that Williams was the devotee of a method of Biblical interpretation which most modern intelligences reject. Hence he came to the problem of freedom not as a disinterested philosopher but as a doctrinaire exponent of a peculiar and highly suspect version of Scripture. Theologically he was an orthodox Calvinist, and like all Calvinists can be accused of Bibliolatry. No one aware of archaeology, textual criticism, historical research, or comparative religion can today so naïvely maintain that the Old Testament is a collection of types of which the New is the antitype, or so rashly look on all nature itself as a typological preaching of Christianity.

Hence the endeavor to understand Williams requires some grasp of his notions of exegesis; if the only reward of such an investigation were to be a familiarity with the typological method, the effort would hardly be worth the making by any except antiquarians. Yet for us the real

meaning of Williams' thought is not the content of his
typology but what, through the practice of it, he came to
demand from society. This was nothing less than that it
respect sincerely held opinions, no matter how bizarre they
might seem to the authorities. Out of the exercise of his
imagination he perceived that no man can be so sure of
any formulation of eternal truth as to have a right to impose on the mind and spirit of other men. Williams further
realized that he who does so impose truth on others is no
longer concerned, in his heart of hearts, with the truth
but only with the imposition. That the social order has
to be maintained, that civil peace must be enforced and
the laws obeyed, he made clear in the letter of 1655. But
what he stood for, and still stands for, is the certainty that
those who mistake their own assurances for divinely appointed missions, and so far forget the sanctity of others'
persuasion as to try reducing them to conformity by physical means, commit in the face of the Divine a sin more
outrageous than any of the statutory crimes.

Or to put it in other words, Roger Williams was a profound Christian who, like Pascal, refused to identify the
Christian vision with worldly appearances, with either any
political order or even the words of the Bible itself.
He knew that the meaning of life lies not on the surface,
but somewhere underneath, and that it must be perpetu-
ally sought. He attacked the political pedant and the textual literalist, not because they are evil men or their motives
not admirable, but because they do not recognize the true
nature of freedom. They lose the essential in the circumstantial, and so deceive themselves into making of their
virtue an instrument of tyranny. They destroy not the
liberty of others but their own.

Hence, in order that men might be protected against the folly of their virtues, Williams insisted on the need for law and order, and at the same time on the utmost allowance within the broad confines of civil peace for every shade of opinion, even the most foolish. By exposing false conceptions of purity and loyalty, he opened the way for a self-distrusting, undogmatic and yet firm resolution to seek for those goals in which alone the soul of man finds fulfillment. So indeed he does remain the symbolic embodiment of that heroism which resists all those who, under whatever slogan, would force the conscience to things it cannot abide. Having bought truth dear, as he says in the best of this prose, we must not sell it cheap, not even for what seems to be the saving of our souls, least of all for the sake of worldly reputation. Wherefore, he was able to contend through a long life for the essential freedom, saying constantly that if he perished, he perished, that eternity would pay for all. In the end, it may be that he is most valuable to us because he incarnates the fighter for ends who keeps always present to his consciousness a sense of his own fallibility, of his own insignificance, without ever for that reason giving over, without ever relaxing, the effort.

Notes

I The Natural Man

1. Of the several modern biographies of Williams, the best in point of factual narrative is Samuel H. Brockunier, *The Irrepressible Democrat: Roger Williams* (New York, 1940); however, it is a particularly sad example of the misrepresentation that comes when Williams is presented too easily in the language of twentieth-century thought.

Other recent biographies, all of them yielding somewhat to the same pressure, are:

Edmund J. Carpenter, *Roger Williams: A Study of the Life, Times and Character of a Political Pioneer* (New York, 1909).

May E. Hall, *Roger Williams* (Boston, 1917).

Emily Easton, *Roger Williams: Prophet and Pioneer* (New York, 1930).

James E. Earnst, *Roger Williams: New England's Firebrand* (New York, 1932).

A new era in Williams scholarship is contained in Mauro Calamandrei's article, "Neglected Aspects of Roger Williams' Thought," *Church History*, XXI (September 1952), 239-259; if this does not answer, it at least poses the essential questions, which of late years have been utterly obscured by the point of view incarnated mainly by Vernon L. Parrington, *Main Currents in American Thought*, I, 62-75, and the liberal biographers.

Most of Williams' books, except those noted below, were reprinted in the six volumes of *The Writings of Roger Williams* (Providence, Rhode Island, Narragansett Club, 1866-1874). Volume VI contains the letters.

II The Evolution of a Prophet

1. For an analysis of the logic of Nonseparation, see my *Orthodoxy in Massachusetts* (Cambridge, 1933).

2. It is true, however, that we have only his word for this call from Boston (see page 239); early records of the church are lost, and no contemporary chronicler mentions it. On the other hand, the silence of later Puritan historians, like Johnson, Hubbard and Cotton Mather, may be deliberate.

3. For Bradford on Williams, see *Of Plymouth Plantation*, ed. Samuel Eliot Morison (New York, 1952), 257,300.

4. Williams' letters to the Winthrops were published in a modernized text in Volume VI of the Narragansett Club issue; they are now being printed in the original and with superb documen-

tation in the Massachusetts Historical Society's edition of *Winthrop Papers*.

5. Since this edition has not yet gone beyond 1649, Williams' letters to Winthrop, Junior, are available only in the Narragansett Club reprint or in earlier volumes of the *Collections* of the Massachusetts Historical Society.

6. Cotton Mather's section on Williams, which is vibrant with suppressed meanings, is in the *Magnalia*, Book VII, Chap. 2.

III PROPHET IN A WILDERNESS

1. See my edition of Jonathan Edwards, *Images or Shadows of Divine Things* (New Haven, 1949).

2. Williams gingerly—and I believe deliberately—sidesteps what has been, for three centuries or more, a difficult problem in Christian evangelism. All churches have had experience with missionaries sent out to convert heathens who have acquired what seemed to the authorities at home too much respect for heathen culture. Williams' implication surely is that he could imagine Indians saved by the Christian God, who yet had never heard the name of Christ.

IV PROPHET IN METROPOLIS

1. See especially Cotton's *A Briefe Exposition of the Whole Book of Canticles* (London, 1642); *A Briefe Exposition with Practicall Observations upon the Whole Book of Ecclesiastes* (London, 1654); *A Brief Exposition with Practical Observations upon the Whole Book of Canticles* (London, 1655). The last two, printed after Cotton's death from manuscripts which probably date from his ministry in England, push the allegorical interpretation to lengths few sober Puritans considered safe.

2. This recapitulation of Tudor history as a meaningless alternation, depending on the accident of the sovereign's inclination, was a favorite theme of Williams'. The modern mind tries to find a logic in the period, in the light of which the personalities of rulers become incidental; but Williams was close to the brutal fact that a Tudor king or queen really did rule, and furthermore, history for him, since the coming of Christ, was full of accident.

3. In his *Reply*, Cotton is vague as to just what was said in these letters, but seems to agree that there were several and challenges Williams to produce them. Why Williams should have lost or suppressed them is a mystery; possibly they might have shown Cotton in a better light than the original letter by itself. However, Cotton was so enraged by the publication—"It may seem by his own words, if he had not found my letter public, it may be doubted whether ever I should have heard any further word from

him hereabout, at all"—that nothing he says in the *Reply* can quite be trusted.

4. See I Chronicles, 13.

5. Undoubtedly Governor Winthrop.

6. This innocent-looking parenthesis was one of Williams' sharpest thrusts: all the sects in England knew by this time that in 1637 Cotton had come perilously close to being expelled along with his adorer, Anne Hutchinson, and had saved himself only at the last moment by abandoning her publicly before the Synod. In the *Reply*, Cotton says that Williams is "falsly and foully misinformed," and tries to tell his version of the miserable business, thus composing some of the most evasive pages ever written by a Puritan.

7. Stephen Gardiner (1483-1555), Bishop of Winchester, as Lord Chancellor under Queen Mary was a vigorous persecutor of Protestants.

8. Edmund Bonner (1500-1569), Bishop of London, was chief advocate of judicial severity against Protestants under Queen Mary; he was deprived of his bishopric on the accession of Elizabeth.

9. For Williams' list of the six fundamentals, see page 115.

10. Williams' marginal note here reveals the basic assumption of his thinking throughout the book, that which becomes fully explicit only in the last portions: "Soul killing the chiefest murder. No magistrate can execute true justice in killing soul for soul but Christ Jesus who, by typical death in the Law, typed out spiritual in the Gospel." The use of "type" as a verb has, of course, a debased connotation in an age which thinks of it only as a performance on a machine; yet even in this modern usage there is a ghostly reminiscence of typology.

11. II Timothy, 2:25.

12. A saker was a piece of ordnance that fired a shot of five pounds and a half; the weapon itself weighed around 1,500 pounds.

13. This passage is one of the best in Williams, entitling him to be hailed as a harbinger of the modern protest against "culture Protestantism."

14. George Buchanan (1506-1582) was a distinguished Scottish humanist, scholar and historian, who from 1570 to 1580 was tutor to King James of Scotland, later James I of England.

15. This refers to the statute of May 18, 1631, when the General Court of Massachusetts Bay limited the colonial franchise to members of the churches in order that "the commons may be preserved of honest and good men." Only about one out of five adult males could thus qualify.

16. Williams had evidently first given Endecott a report on Indian affairs; no matter how estranged he was in thought from the orthodox colonies, he steadily labored for the common peace.

17. A William Hartley, of St. John's College, Oxford, was a Roman Catholic missionary in England and is known to have been associated with the Jesuit Edmund Campion, who was executed in 1581; there is no record outside Williams' passage of an execution of Hartley.

18. The winter of 1651-1652 was exceptionally severe, and the wars had disrupted the flow of coal to London. It is characteristic of Williams that, despite his many responsibilities, he should volunteer to help find fuel for the suffering city.

19. Here is the essence of Williams' controversy with orthodox New England: they insisted that the signs of both God's favor and His disfavor showed that they were a people in covenant with Him. Williams expended himself in their behalf, but refused to regard them as anything other than one among the societies of this earth.

20. See the introduction to *The Hireling Ministry* below.

21. See *The Fourth Paper presented by Major Butler, with other papers edited and published by Roger Williams in London, 1652*, ed. Clarence S. Brigham (Providence, Rhode Island, 1903).

22. On the basis of Acts 17:11, the Christians of Berea have been considered those who most resolutely built their faith and practice entirely on Scripture, without regard to human authority.

23. Thomas Cromwell (1485-1540), Earl of Essex and minister of Henry VIII, administered the policy of dissolving the monasteries and confiscating their lands.

V THE LONG WINTER OF RETIREMENT

1. A facsimile reprint was made at Providence in 1862. A modern edition was prepared by Winthrop J. Hudson, *Experiments of Spiritual Life and Health* (Philadelphia, 1951).

2. The image of a ship was congenial to Williams; he uses it frequently.

3. John Winthrop, Jr., secured the royal charter for Connecticut on May 10, 1662; John Clarke obtained Rhode Island's charter on July 8, 1663.

4. George Fox wrote a reply to Williams, *A New-England Fire-Brand Quenched* (1678), which is compacted of scurrility and vituperation. The second half is subtitled a "Catalogue of R. W.'s envious, malicious, scornful, railing stuff, false accusations and blasphemies, which he foully and unchristian-like hath scattered and dispersed throughout his book, and calls it Scripture-language."

Index

Perry Miller

PERRY G. E. MILLER, Cabot Professor of American Literature at Harvard University, was born at Chicago in 1905. He was educated at the University of Chicago. For his distinguished scholarly work, a number of institutions have conferred honorary degrees upon him, and he has been a Member of the Institute for Advanced Study at Princeton. In addition to the work here presented, his other books include *The New England Mind, the Seventeenth Century; Jonathan Edwards; The New England Mind: From Colony to Province; The Raven and the Whale; Consciousness in Concord.*

Atheneum Paperbacks